WHAT EVERY PRINCIPAL SHOULD KNOW ABOUT

COLLABORATIVE LEADERSHIP

WHAT EVERY PRINCIPAL SHOULD KNOW ABOUT LEADERSHIP
The 7-Book Collection

By Jeffrey Glanz

What Every Principal Should Know About Instructional Leadership

What Every Principal Should Know About Cultural Leadership

What Every Principal Should Know About Ethical and Spiritual Leadership

What Every Principal Should Know About School-Community Leadership

What Every Principal Should Know About Collaborative Leadership

What Every Principal Should Know About Operational Leadership

What Every Principal Should Know About Strategic Leadership

WHAT EVERY PRINCIPAL SHOULD KNOW ABOUT

COLLABORATIVE LEADERSHIP

JEFFREY GLANZ

For information:

Corwin Press
A Sage Publications Company
2455 Teller Road
Thousand Oaks, California 91320
E-mail: order@corwinpress.com

Sage Publications Ltd.
1 Oliver's Yard
55 City Road
London EC1Y 1SP
United Kingdom

Sage Publications India Pvt. Ltd.
B-42, Panchsheel Enclave
Post Box 4109
New Delhi 110 017 India

Printed in the United States of America.

Library of Congress Cataloging-in-Publication Data

Glanz, Jeffrey.
What every principal should know about collaborative leadership / Jeffrey Glanz.
p. cm.
Includes bibliographical references and index.
ISBN 1-4129-1590-2 (pbk.)
1. School principals—United States. 2. Educational leadership—United States. 3. Action research in education—United States. 4. School management and organization—United States. 5. Teacher participation in administration—United States. I. Title.
LB2831.93.G53 2006
371.2′012—dc22

2005013302

This book is printed on acid-free paper.

05 06 07 08 09 10 9 8 7 6 5 4 3 2 1

Acquisitions Editor:	Elizabeth Brenkus
Editorial Assistant:	Candice L. Ling
Production Editor:	Tracy Alpern
Copy Editor:	Rachel Hile Bassett
Proofreader:	Christine Dahlin
Typesetter:	C&M Digitals (P) Ltd.
Indexer:	Gloria Tierney
Cover Designer:	Rose Storey
Graphic Designer:	Scott Van Atta

Contents

To Livingston Alexander, Hal McCulloch, and Devorah Lieberman, who taught me by example the value of collaboration. Also, to Susan Sullivan, Helen Hazi, Linda Behar-Horenstein, and the late Richard Neville, with whom I had the privilege to collaborate on several meaningful projects. Their intellect and insight broadened my intellectual horizons. . . . I remain grateful.

Acknowledgments

Hank Rubin once remarked that "effective collaboration happens between people—one person at a time." Building collaborations among people of diverse interests and abilities isn't easy work. It is essential, though, in order to sustain successful learning communities. Principals that I have been privileged to know and work with have the unique ability to forge political alliances and interpersonal relationships, one on one and with large groups. They realize that building connections takes time and energy. For them, however, the hard work it takes to create partnerships is well worth the efforts extended. Principals are not only visionary and committed, but they are also practical and strategic. Collaborative leadership is a way for them to accomplish their lofty objectives. This book and series are dedicated to all who aspire to the principalship, who currently serve as principals, or who have been principals. No nobler enterprise and profession exists, for principals are the ones who forge partnerships that enhance communication, improve social relationships, and sustain academic excellence throughout the school.

****

Thanks to my acquisitions editor, Lizzie Brenkus, for her gentle encouragement, support, and willingness to help me think things through. Many thanks also go to Robb Clouse, editorial director, who prompted me to consider a trilogy of sorts: a book about teaching, which eventuated into *Teaching 101*; a book about assistant principals, which led to *The Assistant Principal's Handbook*; and a book about principals, which resulted to my surprise in this groundbreaking series, *What Every Principal Should Know About Leadership.*

Special thanks to my wife, Lisa, without whose support such a venture would be impossible. I love you . . . at least as much as I love writing.

Corwin Press gratefully acknowledges the contributions of the following individuals:

Randel Beaver, Superintendent
Archer City Independent
School District
Archer City, TX

Glenn Sewell,
Superintendent/Principal
Wheatland Union
High School District
Wheatland, CA

Bonnie Tryon, Principal
Golding Elementary School
Cobleskill, NY

Steve Zsiray,
Associate Superintendent
Cache County
School District
North Logan, UT

About the Author

Jeffrey Glanz, EdD, currently serves as Dean of Graduate Programs and Chair of the Department of Education at Wagner College in Staten Island, New York. He also coordinates the educational leadership program that leads to New York State certification as a principal or assistant principal. Prior to arriving at Wagner, he served as executive assistant to the president of Kean University in Union, New Jersey. Dr. Glanz held faculty status as a tenured professor in the Department of Instruction and Educational Leadership at Kean University's College of Education. He was named Graduate Teacher of the Year in 1999 by the Student Graduate Association and was also that year's recipient of the Presidential Award for Outstanding Scholarship. He served as an administrator and teacher in the New York City public schools for 20 years. Dr. Glanz has authored, coauthored, or coedited 13 books and has more than 35 peer-reviewed article publications. With Corwin Press he coauthored the bestselling *Supervision That Improves Teaching* (2nd ed.) and *Supervision in Practice: Three Steps to Improve Teaching and Learning* and authored *The Assistant Principal's Handbook* and *Teaching 101: Strategies for the Beginning Teacher.* More recently he coauthored *Building Effective Learning Communities: Strategies for Leadership, Learning, & Collaboration.* Most recently, Dr. Glanz has authored *What Every Principal Should Know About Leadership: The 7-Book Collection*:

What Every Principal Should Know About Instructional Leadership

What Every Principal Should Know About Cultural Leadership

What Every Principal Should Know About Ethical and Spiritual Leadership

What Every Principal Should Know About School-Community Leadership

What Every Principal Should Know About Collaborative Leadership

What Every Principal Should Know About Operational Leadership

What Every Principal Should Know About Strategic Leadership

Consult his Web site for additional information: http://www.wagner.edu/faculty/users/jglanz/web/.

* * * * * * * * * * * * * * * *

The "About the Author" information you've just glanced at (excuse the pun . . . my name? . . . Glanz, "glance"?!) is standard author bio info you find in most books. As you'll discover if you glance at . . . I mean *read* . . . the Introduction, I want this book to be user-friendly in several ways. One of the ways is that I want to write as I would converse with you in person. Therefore, I prefer in most places to use the first person, so please excuse the informality. Although we've likely never met, we really do know each other if you think about it. We share a common passion about leadership, school building leadership to be more precise. We share many similar experiences. In an experiential, almost spiritual, sense, we have much in common. What I write about directly relates, I hope, to your lived experience. The information in this volume, as with the entire series, is meant to resonate, stir, provoke, and provide ideas about principal leadership, which is vital in order to promote excellence and achievement for all.

This traditional section of a book is titled "About the Author." The first paragraph in this section tells you what I "do," not "about" me or who I am. I won't bore you with all details "about me," but I'd like just to share one bit of info that communicates more meaningfully about "me" than the information in the first paragraph. I am (I presume like you) passionate about what I do. I love to teach, guide, mentor, learn, supervise, and lead. For me, leadership is self-preservation. Personally and professionally, I strive to do my very best, to use whatever God-given leadership talents I possess to make a difference in the lives of others. I continually strive to improve myself intellectually and socially, but also physically and spiritually. I realize that I cannot lead alone. Leadership is a shared responsibility. My success as a leader depends on building and maintaining collaborative relationships with others. Leadership is too complex to go it alone. Collaborative leadership is imperative.

If any of the information in this book series touches you in any way, please feel free to contact me by using my personal e-mail address: tora.dojo@verizon.net. I encourage you to share your reactions, comments, and suggestions, or simply to relate an anecdote or two, humorous or otherwise, that may serve as "information from the field" for future editions of this work, ultimately to help others. Your input is much appreciated.

Questionnaire: Before We Get Started . . .

Directions: Using the Likert scale below, circle the answer that best represents your on-the-spot belief about each statement. The questionnaire serves as an advanced organizer of sorts for some of the key topics in this book, although items are purposely constructed in no particular order. Discussion of each topic, though, occurs within the context of relevant chapters. Responses or views to each statement are presented in a subsection following the questionnaire (this section begins "Now, let's analyze your responses . . ."). You may or may not agree with the points made, but I hope you will be encouraged to reflect on your own views. Reflective activities follow to allow for deeper analysis. Elaboration of ideas emanating from this brief activity will occur throughout the text and series. I encourage you to share reflections (yours and mine) with colleagues. I'd appreciate your personal feedback via the e-mail address I've listed in the "About the Author" section.

SA = Strongly Agree ("For the most part, yes.")
A = Agree ("Yes, but . . .")
D = Disagree ("No, but . . .")
SD = Strongly Disagree ("For the most part, no.")

SA A D SD 1. Principals value collaboration because they realize that the more minds working on a project, the greater the likelihood for its success.

SA A D SD 2. Collaborative decision making should be incorporated whenever a significant decision has to be made.

SA A D SD 3. Most decisions should be made by committee vote and not by the principal alone.

SA A D SD 4. It's possible to fake collaboration.

SA A D SD 5. Democracy demands collaboration.

SA A D SD 6. Collaboration and competition are like oil and water; they don't mix.

SA A D SD 7. Collaborative leadership involves consensus building and diplomacy.

SA A D SD 8. It is possible for administrators and faculty to develop mutual trust and respect for each other as well as share common beliefs that focus on student learning.

SA A D SD 9. The principal is the key person in a school to encourage a team or school spirit.

SA A D SD 10. Schools can learn much from collaborative enterprises in business.

SA A D SD 11. *Collegiality* and *collaboration* are pretty much synonymous terms.

SA A D SD 12. An effective principal can encourage meaningful collaboration within a relatively short period of time, say, six months.

SA A D SD 13. I have been involved in some team-building activity within the past six months.

SA A D SD 14. I have been involved in some sort of shared decision-making process within the past six months.

SA A D SD 15. I have been involved in some sort of collaborative action research project within the past six months.

Before we analyze your responses, consider the fact that schooling in the 21st century is more complicated than ever. The headmaster or principal of yesteryear who single-handedly was able to monitor, oversee, and manage all school operations is no longer viable or even a possibility. Roles and responsibilities of principals have expanded. In the current world of heightened accountability, principals are challenged to manage and lead not only larger schools but also ones more diverse than ever. Most recently, many school systems have given over fiscal or budgetary responsibilities to principals. Schools, as in the past, continue to care for children socially, emotionally, physically, as well as instructionally. Teachers, too, are required to handle much more than in the past. Teachers and principals by themselves cannot manage the ever-changing educational landscape. The nostalgic notion or image of the teacher (e.g., Nick Nolte in *Teachers*) or the evangelical (some might say maniacal) image of the principal (e.g., Joe Clark in *Lean on Me*) who almost single-handedly combat social and political forces that "win the day" is naive at best, given the complexities educators face in schools today. The notion of principal as "white knight" riding on a "white horse" to "save the day" is ludicrous, if not unrealistic. In short, collaboration is more important than ever.

But have we been taught to be collaborative? Most of us haven't. We've been raised in a culture that values independence and the "go it alone" attitude. These cultural images of an independent leader are embedded and reinforced through television, film, and other forms of media (see, e.g., Spring, 1992). When we do reach out to others, it is usually because we need something, not because we value others' viewpoints to better inform our own. We may realize that no single individual can "go it alone," but we need to develop the skills necessary to make collaboration work. These skills or mind-sets might include, among others, the ability to listen to others' viewpoints; the willingness to let go of a dogmatically held view in order to achieve consensus with others; the realization that solutions developed collaboratively almost always turn out better than decisions made by just one person; the ability to negotiate, coach, and problem-solve, and so forth.

A collaborative leader, therefore

- realizes that schools are too complex for one person to make all the decisions;

- thinks about different ways of involving others in school policies;
- shares information with others who have a stake in the particular activity;
- listens;
- encourages, trains, and coaches others to participate in schoolwide, subject-specific, or grade-level decision making;
- forms committees that are empowered to make important curricular and instructional decisions;
- solicits the advice of teachers and others;
- reaches out on a daily basis to parents, students, school secretaries, custodians, specialized support staff, and, of course, teachers;
- believes that collaborative leadership is a moral imperative for a principal in the 21st century;
- engages the school staff and community in training to help better understand collaborative decision making.

As you consider the meaning and relevance of collaborative leadership, share your thoughts about these questions with a colleague:

Reflective Questions

1. Do you really believe collaboration results in better decisions? Under all circumstances? If not, in which situations would you find collaboration appealing?
2. Is there any value to collaborative decision making even though the decision that results may not be as good as you alone might make? Explain.
3. How would you respond to a colleague who proclaims that "collaboration is a waste of time since it's the principal who ultimately has to make important decisions . . . collaboration simply wastes valuable time"?
4. What does collaborative leadership mean to you, and why is it so important, if it is? Explain.
5. What are specific ways you solicit collaboration in your school?

* * * * * * * * * * * * * * * *

Examine these quotations on collaboration. What do they mean to you?

> *"Today's effective principal . . . participates in collaborative practices . . . it is much easier to tell or to manage than it is to perform as a collaborative instructional leader."*
>
> —Linda Lambert

> *"The relationships among adults in schools are the basis, the precondition, the sine qua non that allow, energize, and sustain all other attempts at school improvement. Unless adults talk with one another, observe one another, and help one another, very little will change."*
>
> —Roland S. Barth

> *"The leadership style which had the greatest impact on teacher morale was collaborative."*
>
> —Vernadine Thomas

> *"Collaboration . . . has emerged as the cornerstone for discussions about supervision in education. We believe that the call for collaboration is more than ideological. Learning requires a collaborative effort between student and teacher. In this respect, collaboration can be thought of as the dominant value driving the organization of schooling."*
>
> —James E. Barott and Patrick F. Galvin

> *"It is incumbent upon a principal to serve as a role model for collegiality and foster such relationships among teachers and staff members through a clear focus on student learning."*
>
> —Marsha Speck

> *"The 'collaborative premise' is a belief that 'if you bring the appropriate people together in constructive ways with good information, they will create authentic visions and strategies*

for addressing the shared concerns of the organization or community.'"

—David D. Chrislip and
Carl E. Larson, as cited by Susan R. Komives,
Nance Lucas, and Timothy R. McMahon

"The wise leader is he who the people despise. The good leader is he who the people revere. The great leader is he who the people say, 'We did it ourselves.'"

—Lao Tsu

* * * * * * * * * * * * * * * *

Now, let's analyze your responses to the questionnaire:

1. Principals value collaboration because they realize that the more minds working on a project, the greater the likelihood for its success.

Successful principals gather others for input in matters of instructional importance. Decisions about a choice of new science textbooks, for example, cannot be made by principal and supervisor of science alone. Input from teachers, students, and parents is advisable. Teachers as a group may offer insights that parents or administrators may not have contemplated. Soliciting the views of students will help you gather evidence from those individuals who will ultimately be using the text. As principal, you realize that any decision made will be stronger, more accepted, and more viable if input from others is obtained. Certainly, the easier thing to do is to order the texts yourself, especially if you've had experience with them in another school, perhaps in some other district. It would not, however, be the wise choice.

Collaboration can also be evidenced in matters with more impact on the school as a whole. For instance, creating or revising curriculum policies should be accomplished with the input of key instructional leaders and others in the school. Principals committed to collaboration take the time to convene a group of curriculum leaders, students, and parents to review instructional materials and curriculum guidelines. Teams of educators can be convened to decide whether or not, for instance, to adopt a new schoolwide Balanced Literacy program. In matters of instructional or curricular issues, successful principals build bridges, include others, and communicate a team approach or "collaborative" spirit in the school.

2. Collaborative decision making should be incorporated whenever a significant decision has to be made.

Collaborative decision making is time-consuming. If you are not committed to such leadership, you will not likely invite input, especially under pressure situations (e.g., you receive a call from the superintendent saying she needs an immediate decision about some budgetary matter). Even if you fervently believe in collaboration, you realize that collaborating on simple, everyday matters is unnecessary. Deciding to call the local Emergency Medical Team in the event that one of the students is bleeding profusely is a no-brainer. Similarly, you wouldn't call together the School-Based Leadership Team to call a fire drill. However, in which of the following matters would you involve others in a formal way: deciding on a new literacy approach for fifth-grade students, hiring a new kindergarten teacher, spending $100,000 in newly obtained grant initiatives, or implementing an intervisitation supervisory approach? One could posit that each of the aforementioned matters is significant enough to warrant collaborative decision making. Others might accede to involving others in curricular, instructional, and even budgetary matters; however, hiring is another issue entirely. Some principals believe that such matters are solely within their purview. Some principals might argue that it is indeed wise to involve others in hiring decisions, not only because of the benefits of having different perspectives but, more important, to foster a collaborative spirit in the school. Involving others (teachers, parents, and students) demonstrates that you, as principal, "walk the talk" when it comes to collaborative leadership. Such efforts bridge the proverbial gap between espoused theory and theory-in-use (Osterman & Kottkamp, 2004). Principals foster collaboration by their actions and their deeds, not merely by what they espouse.

3. Most decisions should be made by committee vote and not by the principal alone.

Thus far, we've discussed some benefits of collaborative leadership and some situations in which collaborative decision making might make sense. However, who makes the ultimate decision? In other words, involving others is one thing, but giving them a vote in decision making is quite another. One principal I worked with put it this way: "I am in favor of collaboration; I mean, giving teachers and parents voice, but darned if I'm going to let them usurp my authority. Ultimately, I am accountable, not a committee." Another principal shared her view: "Why not give others voting power? If we don't we're giving lip service to collaboration. In the end, whatever decision is made will likely be better than any one individual can make. In fact, giving a committee voting authority communicates schoolwide ownership to a given problem or issue." If you indeed believe in collaborative leadership, it's important for you to decide in advance which matters you would leave for committee vote and which matters you would retain for yourself. You might, for instance, decide that for some matters you would concede to committee vote, for others you would solicit committee input while retaining final decision making for yourself, yet for still other matters you would reserve the right to make a decision independent of others. In this latter situation, make sure you fully explain your rationale so that your views are understood and not confused with a noncollaborative stance.

4. It's possible to fake collaboration.

One may espouse a commitment to collaboration, but one's actions may belie such a stance. Faculty will listen respectfully to you articulate your vision of collaborative leadership, but they will postpone judgment until they see you in action. Do you indeed consult with them? Whom do you consult with? What decision-making authority do you give others? Who really makes the decisions? Do they feel a part of the school's vision and goals for the future? As principal, you must ensure a congruence between your espoused theory and your theory-in-use (Osterman & Kottkamp, 2004). A disconnect doesn't necessarily occur intentionally. In other words, few principals would intentionally "fake" collaboration. The point here is to closely monitor what you espouse and how you act.

5. Democracy demands collaboration.

Collaboration is premised most fundamentally on relationships that are governed by democratic principles. Meaningful and collegial relations are supported and encouraged by democratic values. Rubin (2002) states that "collaboration is democracy's mandate" (p. 4). Further, he admonishes us:

> *Collaboration is almost always more time-consuming and challenging than is acting on one's own because collaboration requires skills*

> *most of us were never taught, and because a collaborative way of thinking conflicts with the traditional structures and reward systems in which nearly all of us routinely work. So we all have found ourselves trying to avoid collaboration, diminishing its central importance, doing it poorly, or defensively dismissing it as an external mandate—something we do simply because funders and regulatory agencies tell us we must. This is a big mistake. (p. 5)*

Effective principals believe in participative democracy. They actively solicit input on a range of school-related issues. Collaborative or participative leadership is concerned with decision-making processes, establishing priorities within a school, and collectively developing strategies to accomplish mutually agreed-upon goals and objectives.

6. Collaboration and competition are like oil and water; they don't mix.

Not true. Using a sports analogy, Rubin (2002) explains that viewing the terms as two opposites is a "false dichotomy." He explains that "even the most solitary of individual sports requires deep and sustained partnerships among athletes, coaches, and sponsors in order to succeed" (p. 10). He admonishes us by saying:

> *Until we place as much value on collaboration as we do on competition, we will (1) perpetuate the false dichotomy, (2) justify devaluation of collaboration and civic education as things that children should be taught in school, and (3) continue to produce only those rare coaches and citizens who really understand how to build collaborative teams. (pp. 10–11)*

7. Collaborative leadership involves consensus building and diplomacy.

Yes, and much more. Collaborative work means that principals build trust and rapport with colleagues. They establish solid relationships and influence school culture through relationships (York-Barr & Duke, 2004). Rubin (2002) elaborates on what he calls "dimensions of collaborative leadership." These dimensions include, among others, strategic thinking, group process, systems thinking, and a commitment to diversity. More specifically, consensus building, according to Rubin, involves five principles:

- *If you can't be clear on the intended outcome, be clear on the question you want answered. Our job, as collaborative leaders, is to move our group step-by-step toward our goals . . . our best role may be to pose questions that evoke the distillation of complex issues into bite-size achievable decisions around which we can facilitate consensus-building discussion.*

- *See the world through the eyes of those you would influence. . . .*

- *Our job . . . beckons us to be persistent, push for consensus, and persist in shaping and adapting the question and the environment until (finally) a satisfying decision that responds to our colleagues' self-interests can be reached.*

- *Be an advocate for the collaboration, not for any one decision. As collaborative leaders, we are the ones who are most invested in the health and success of the collaboration. And, while passions may run high on any one question or decision facing our group, we should be the ones to whom our colleagues can turn for leadership and advocacy on behalf of the whole collaboration. Collaborative leaders have a duty to be cautious of when and how we advocate specific policy positions or courses of action within our collaborations. . . .*

- *Ask for and isolate the objection. Narrow the focus of the conflict until it is clearly identified and isolated. Then present the objection clearly to ensure its validity for both parties. (pp. 64–65)*

Collaborative leadership also involves diplomacy. As principal, you should act the role of the diplomat. Speak to all parties involved, solicit their input, and listen. When different opinions exist, serve as the negotiator by striving for a win-win position. Bring parties together many times in an open, facilitative environment of trust and collegiality. Finally, give credit to each individual who participated in achieving consensus.

8. It is possible for administrators and faculty to develop mutual trust and respect for each other as well as share common beliefs that focus on student learning.

Such goals are not only possible, they are imperative. Too often, administrators and faculty are pitted against each other, especially in unionized environments. Without taking a stand on unionization and the education profession, we need to nurture collaborative relationships for the benefit of the children attending schools. The focus of all our efforts, ultimately, must be on student learning. Collaborative leadership, in this context, focuses on these questions, among others: What partnerships are necessary to best promote student achievement? How can teachers and administrators work together for the benefit of student learning? What else do teachers and administrators have in common? How might they forge meaningful, collegial relationships?

9. The principal is the key person in a school to encourage a team or school spirit.

No doubt about it. You, as principal, are essential for advocating, organizing, and monitoring collaboration schoolwide. You certainly cannot collaborate alone. You are, however, key. What are you prepared to do to achieve meaningful collaboration or team spirit? Why is it so important for you?

10. Schools can learn much from collaborative enterprises in business.

We must reach out to all quarters of the community, and certainly building partnerships with local businesses is essential. Although we can learn much from the way businesses foster cooperation and collaboration, we, as educators, have a rich history of collaboration of our own. What schools have you worked in, visited, or heard about that may serve as models for the kind of collaboration you want to nurture? Why does collaboration work there, and can you somehow replicate their experiences? What modifications might you have to make?

11. *Collegiality* and *collaboration* are pretty much synonymous terms.

According to Rubin (2002), collaboration *"is a purposeful relationship in which all parties strategically choose to cooperate in order to accomplish a shared outcome" (p. 17). Collaboration can be conceived of, then, as an intentional process in which a group of individuals unites for a common goal. Cooperation is the mechanism by which they accomplish their goal. Collegiality, then, may be viewed as an outcome of working collaboratively.*

Robbins and Alvy (2003) remind us that "collegiality that exists when staff members collaborate is not created overnight" (p. 140). They discuss the importance of congeniality as a step toward meaningful collaboration. Congeniality, they explain, is "designed to create a sense of comfort with one another as human beings" (p. 141). Getting together after work to share a beer or meet at a faculty member's home to socialize builds a sense of congeniality. It's not necessary, though, that staff members become close friends. Rather, the point is to develop and nurture a sense of friendliness and willingness to work together to solve common problems or address mutual issues.

12. An effective principal can encourage meaningful collaboration within a relatively short period of time, say, six months.

Meaningful collaborative relationships take time and cannot be time-tabled. Don't worry about having to meet some arbitrary deadline. Work first to build trust and rapport among faculty and staff. Establish mechanisms that encourage meaningful communication. Develop a people-oriented stance. Get out there on a daily basis. Don't let paperwork bog you down. Set aside other times for what we all know is "administrivia," that is, those logistical or administrative matters that must be done but that distract us from the work that will truly make a difference.

13. I have been involved in some team-building activity within the past six months.

Those of us who have, in fact, worked as collegial partners on various educational projects are in a good position to truly understand the commitments and hard work involved in such work. Not having served on strategic planning committees or schoolwide leadership councils, as examples, may put staff members at a disadvantage. Learning to work with others is a skill we must teach and not assume that people possess. Team-building activities aimed at encouraging group cohesiveness, efficiency, and on-task behavior are essential. Collaborative leaders are familiar with several team-building strategies and techniques in order to ensure that people work cooperatively toward some mutually dependent common goal (Biech, 2001).

14. I have been involved in some sort of shared decision-making process within the past six months.

Those of you who have served successfully on shared decision-making teams or committees are in a good position to model congenial, cooperative, and collaborative working relationships. One of the toughest things to overcome on such committees is the idea of letting go of a firmly held position in order to accommodate another's perspective. Experience in having done so is critical for the collaborative leader. Principals who have experienced, firsthand, shared decision-making opportunities will more likely encourage the same in their schools.

15. I have been involved in some sort of collaborative action research project within the past six months.

Similar experiences are important. Collaborative action research is a unique form of collaboration, one we will discuss in more detail in Chapter 3.

Reflective Questions

1. Which of the explanations above make the most sense to you?
2. Which of the explanations above make the least sense to you? Explain why.
3. Can you think of an instance when collaboration did not fare well at your school? Explain how you resolved or might resolve the situation.
4. Can you think of a school situation that may be significant but in which you would not solicit the opinion of others? Explain.
5. In what ways do you collaborate with teachers? Parents? Students? Community representatives? Explain with details.
6. Recall principals you know or have known who are involved in meaningful, ongoing collaborative efforts. Are they people you would want to emulate? Explain.

See "Resources" sections for more detailed surveys to assess your knowledge of teamwork, action research, and shared decision making. Rather than presenting a single survey on collaborative leadership, as used in some of the other volumes in this series on the principalship, I've divided the survey into three distinct ones reflecting the content of each of the chapters in this book. See Resource B for a survey involving teamwork, Resource C for one on action research, and Resource D for one on shared decision making.

CHAPTER ONE

Introduction

"The old leadership model—in other words, just being a manager—doesn't work. . . . Now school leaders have to know teaching inside and out. They have to know best practices. They have to know how to structure a school to support teaching and learning. They have to know about professional development for ongoing learning—job-embedded, collaborative types of learning."

—Wendy Katz

This book represents one aspect of a principal's work. Each book in the series addresses a specific, important role or function of a principal. Discussing each separately, however, is quite artificial and a bit contrived. In fact, all seven forms of leadership (instructional, cultural, ethical/spiritual, school-community, operational, strategic, and collaborative) that make up this series of *What Every Principal Should Know About . . .* form an undifferentiated whole. To talk about, for instance, collaboration without understanding the cultural context in which it occurs is shortsighted and limiting. School culture and climate impact the nature and form of collaboration within a particular school.

The work of Hargreaves and Dawe (1989) is relevant in this context. They discuss four types of cultures that may influence the degree or extent to which collaboration takes place in a school:

1. *Fragmented individualism*—Often representing the traditional conception of school governance, the cultural milieu of fragmented

individualism operates with the principal as authoritative overseer of a group of individual teachers who work in isolation of each other. Information is communicated in a top-down fashion, often by administrative fiat. Relationships are usually impersonal and bureaucratic. Teaching and learning are often viewed as simple processes in which teachers transfer knowledge to passive learners. The school functions in predictable, fixed ways. Individuality is subservient to organizational needs and demands.

2. *Balkanization*—Similar to fragmented individualism, the cultural milieu of balkanization operates in a competitive environment in which subgroups within the organization vie for resources. Disparate, disjointed cliques operate in isolation of one another and with the school at large. Few schoolwide improvement initiatives ever have a chance of succeeding within this fragmented environment.

3. *Contrived collegiality*—Although this is not the place to discuss this concept at length, one essential premise involves the notion that a sense of collegiality is attempted with few, if any, long-lasting positive results for both the participants or the organization. A principal, for instance, might feign collegiality or collaboration by forming a committee to distribute educational resources. But in the end, the principal may have complete veto or decision-making authority to overrule or simply ignore committee decisions. Such efforts at collegial relations might offer some sort of temporary personal benefits to the participants (e.g., some time out of the classroom to meet), but often these benefits are ephemeral and certainly not influential on a schoolwide scale.

4. *True collaborative cultures*—In this ideal cultural milieu, teachers and administrators may form "deep personal" (Hargreaves & Dawe, 1989, p. 14) relationships that enhance the school in significant ways. In such an environment, personal relationships are fostered within a learning community. Diversity is appreciated and fostered throughout the school. Problem solving is seen as a schoolwide responsibility, although no easy solutions may be at hand. It is only through deep personal commitments to work together that solutions can surface. Teaching and learning are engaging, complex enterprises. A sense of self-efficacy is affirmed, and individuality is valued above the needs of the organization. Leadership is distributed, situational, and ongoing.

It is within this latter cultural milieu that this book is framed. Collaborative leadership reflects an educational paradigm based on the following assumptions:

- You, as principal, play the most vital role in facilitating (i.e., establishing and sustaining) such a cultural milieu.
- Quality education for all depends on quality learning for educators.
- Learning is complex and differentiated.
- Educators participate as collegial partners to enhance school/classroom improvement.
- Diversity is appreciated and celebrated, and cultural understanding among all people in a free, democratic society is supported.
- Educational leadership emerges for all quarters of the school organization.
- Educational leaders are willing to take risks, seek innovation, and work as transformative leaders in order to promote student learning.
- Educators have a moral responsibility to make a difference in the lives of their students, promoting high achievement for all.
- Schools cannot improve without the systematic and ongoing participation of the many. (See, e.g., Glanz & Sullivan, 2000.)

Reflective Questions

1. Consider leaders you have known. Assess their collaborative leadership skills. What stands out as particularly noteworthy? Unworthy?
2. Assess the degree to which a "true collaborative culture" exists in your school. How can you contribute to a more collegial, cooperative, and collaborative climate?
3. What collaborative leadership challenges do you face? Explain.
4. React to the nine assumptions listed above. Which make the most sense to you?

* * * * * * * * * * * * * * * *

The major themes of this book and series on the principalship are as follows:

• The principal models collaborative leadership in all aspects of a school's work. Collaboration is necessary in order to best meet the ever-increasing demands placed on schools, and specifically on the principal. To the extent that you, as principal, foster a sense of esprit de corps, you will likely succeed in your endeavors. As Robbins and Alvy (2003) succinctly state, "a key factor in the development of a collaborative school is the principal's role" (p. 145).

• Collaborative leadership is instrumental in fostering a democratic learning community. The work of Sergiovanni (1994) is as instructive as it is relevant. Democratic communities embrace collaboration as a chief way to involve others in an active citizenry. Sergiovanni explains:

> Active citizenship forces everyone to get into each other's pockets by requiring them to come to grips with a collective image of school life, to work together to solve problems, to invest together in the welfare of the community, and to live together in accordance with community norms. (p. 123)

Sergiovanni continues, "In a democratic community, the official culture is not imposed by one on another but is created together." Sergiovanni underscores the commitment we all must have to ensure that meaningful collaboration occurs. He states, "Democratic communities make demands on all of their members. Teachers, administrators, and students all have obligations and duties to each other and to the school that must be met." He concludes, "These demands let members know that they are needed by the community and belong to the community, thus further solidifying the ties that bind and bond" (p. 123).

• Fostering positive, ongoing, and meaningful collaboration takes much time and commitment, but the rewards are monumental. When collaboration works, ownership of programs and practices schoolwide is a shared responsibility. Fault lies with no single individual. Problems are seen from an institutional or organizational perspective. Problem solving becomes a group responsibility. Moreover, in a collaborative school atmosphere, failure is viewed as a step towards success. Collaboration promotes positive thinking and a sense of optimism that pervades the entire school.

- To many, collaboration is "the single most important factor" for successful schooling (Newmann & Wehlage, 1995, as quoted in Robbins & Alvy, 2003, p. 146). Robbins and Alvy explain further that "schools that are able to reach such a state report a sense of synergy, creativity, and a capacity for innovation and learning uncommon to those who function in isolation" (p. 146).

This book and series are also aligned with standards established by the prominent Educational Leadership Constituent Council (ELCC). ELCC standards are commonly accepted by most educational organizations concerned with preparing high-quality educational leaders and as such are most authoritative (Wilmore, 2002). The ELCC, an arm of the National Council for the Accreditation of Teacher Education, developed six leadership standards used widely in principal preparation. These standards formed the basis for this book and series:

*1.0: Candidates who complete the program are educational leaders who have the knowledge and ability to promote the success of all students by facilitating the development, articulation, implementation, and stewardship of a school or district vision of learning supported by the school community.

2.0: Candidates who complete the program are educational leaders who have the knowledge and ability to promote the success of all students by promoting a positive school culture, providing an effective instructional program, applying best practices to student learning, and designing comprehensive professional growth plans for staff.

3.0: Candidates who complete the program are educational leaders who have the knowledge and ability to promote the success of all students by managing the organization, operations, and resources in a way that promotes a safe, efficient, and effective learning environment.

*4.0: Candidates who complete the program are educational leaders who have the knowledge and ability to promote the success of all students by collaborating with families and other community members, responding to diverse community interests and needs, and mobilizing community resources.

5.0: Candidates who complete the program are educational leaders who have the knowledge and ability to promote the success of all students by acting with integrity, fairly, and in an ethical manner.

6.0: Candidates who complete the program are educational leaders who have the knowledge and ability to promote the success of all students by understanding, responding to, and influencing the larger political, social, economic, legal, and cultural context.

* This standard is addressed in this book.

Readers should also familiarize themselves with standards from the Interstate School Leaders Licensure Consortium, the National Association of Elementary School Principals, and the National Association of Secondary School Principals (see, e.g., http://www.ccsso.org/projects/Interstate_School_Leaders_Licensure_Consortium/, http://www.boyercenter.org/basicschool/naesp.shtml, and http://www.nassp.org/s_nassp/index.asp).

Another important point to make in this introduction is for you to realize that although with other forms of leadership (e.g., instructional, operational, and strategic), you must take specific actions to address them, and at times you don't actually have to actively engage in them, as a collaborative leader you are continually interacting with others by advising, coaching, sharing, visioning, and partnering all day long. Your daily activities, actions, memoranda, e-mails, formal and informal meetings, personal contacts, decisions, and so forth reflect, shape, and influence your role as collaborative leader.

Reflective Questions

1. Which of the themes or core values above make the most sense to you?
2. Which of the themes or core values above make the least sense to you? Explain.

3. How do you perceive your role as collaborative leader? What specific actions must you take to be effective? Be specific.
4. What do you do on a daily basis that affirms your commitment to collaborative leadership? Provide details with examples.

****

In order to establish a framework for the three main chapters, it is important to understand the "Three-Phase Collaborative Leadership Model for Whole-School Improvement" (see Figure 1.1), which serves as the conceptual framework for *What Every Principal Should Know About Collaborative Leadership.* This book does not purport to present the definitive work on principal collaborative leadership. Rather, a more modest objective is intended. In order to provide you, the reader, with a beginning, yet solid, framework for establishing collaborative leadership, I have developed this three-phase approach.

Team building, action research, and shared decision making are three, although not the only, vital components of any collaborative leadership initiative. The principal, as collaborative leader, initiates or generates interest in collaboration by word and deed. Research-based team-building strategies are particularly effective for training staff in collaborative beliefs and behaviors. Although ongoing and fully integrated, as Figure 1.1 demonstrates with the use of arrows, team-building techniques are a good way to start building support for schoolwide collaboration. Participants learn, among other things, how to work as a team through negotiation, compromise, and consensus building. Developing deep personal commitments to the institutional mission is of utmost concern. Forging personal friendships, although nice, is not necessary. Team building will create an atmosphere in which education professionals learn how to coordinate and cooperate for the benefit of all students and for the school as a whole.

Once a degree of teaming is achieved, the principal can initiate action research projects aimed at grade-level or whole-school issues. Action research, a disciplined inquiry used by practitioners to solve everyday problems, is an excellent (and research-based) strategy that reflects and supports collaboration. During the

Figure 1.1 A Three-Phase Collaborative Leadership Model for Whole-School Improvement

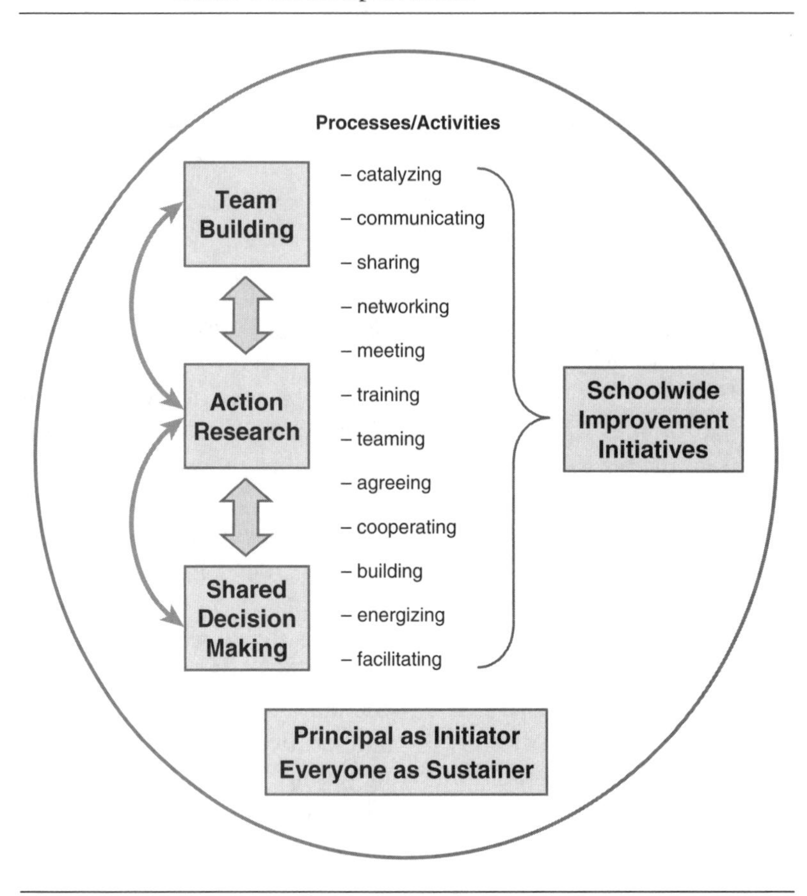

action research cycle, participants identify problems, usually instructional, to solve. After data are collected and analyzed, conclusions are drawn. Action guidelines are then identified for implementation and field testing. The action research cycle is cyclical. A collaborative team (at a grade level or on a schoolwide basis) could undertake, for instance, action research in order to inform decision making regarding the new literature-based reading series.

The third phase represents an attempt to encourage shared decision making, a critical aspect of collaborative leadership.

Although participants may have been involved in ongoing team-building practice and action research committee work, the knowledge and skills necessary to function as decision makers are unique. As Figure 1.1 indicates, all three phases relate to one another on an ongoing basis. Although the principal may initiate collaboration, eventual success depends on everyone's input. Collaboration cannot be mandated by fiat, nor can it be controlled by the principal. Buy-in by the staff is necessary for its success. Although the principal might encourage participation, facilitate meetings, encourage communication, and develop reward mechanisms, it is the ultimate responsibility of the participants to ensure that the initiative is sustained. When these phases work at their best and problems are addressed at the systemic level, the outcome is whole-school improvement.

Allow me to offer a word on chapter format and presentation of information. Information in each of the three main chapters is presented as concisely as possible to make for easy and quick reference reading. Each chapter begins with boxed material called "What You Should Know About." The box will list and briefly explain the concepts covered in each chapter. Certainly, each chapter will not cover every bit of information there is to know about a given topic, as mentioned earlier. Each chapter culls, though, essential knowledge, skills, and dispositions necessary for a successful principal.

A brief word on chapter organization is in order to facilitate reading. The first chapter includes some best practices for helping you create team spirit via use of selected team-building techniques. After this introduction to some of these practical strategies that form the basis for future collaborations, the second chapter reviews best practices for fostering collaborative action research in order to promote student learning and organizational effectiveness. The final chapter highlights best practices for establishing, facilitating, and assessing shared decision-making opportunities. Engaging and encouraging collaborative decision making is the heart of collaborative leadership. Taken together, these three chapters provide you with information and strategies that promote a sense of collaborative inquiry. This book is not meant to be the definitive treatise on collaborative leadership, but rather to raise some relevant issues for your consideration. It is my hope that the ideas in this book will give you pause to think about your own collaborative style in your interactions with others and encourage you to ponder some of the best ways to promote collegiality and cooperation among faculty and staff.

As a concluding activity to this Introduction, read the boxed material below, which contains 10 quotations meant to inspire, but more importantly to provoke critical thinking about your role as collaborative leader. Read each quotation and ask yourself these questions:

- What does the author convey about collaboration, directly or indirectly (in other words, what's the message in a nutshell)?
- Critique the quotation. Does the thought reflect your beliefs? Explain.
- What practical step(s) could you take to actualize the idea behind each quotation?

Some Key Quotations Related to Collaborative Leadership

"The purpose of collaboration is to create a shared vision and joint strategies to address concerns that go beyond the purview of any particular party."

—David D. Chrislip and Carl E. Larson

"A learning organization is an organization in which people at all levels are, collectively, continually enhancing their capacity to create things they really want to create."

—Peter Senge

"Leadership is not something possessed only by a select few people in high positions. We are all involved in the leadership process, and we are all capable of being effective leaders. Through collaboration with others, you can make a difference."

—Susan R. Komives, Nance Lucas, and Timothy R. McMahon

"When we choose co-creation [collaboration], we end separation, the root cause of conflict. . . . They know through responsible participation that they can empower each other and ultimately their institutions and society, thereby creating a life that is meaningful and satisfying for everyone."

—Thomas F. Crum

"It's a mistake to go it alone. By creating alliances even before your initiative becomes public, you can increase the probability that both you and your ideas will succeed. For the next meeting, personally make the advance phone calls, test the waters, refine your approach, and line up supporters. . . . Know their existing alliances and loyalties so you realize how far you are asking them to stretch to collaborate with you."

—Ronald A. Heifetz and Marty Linsky

"Time is a precious resource in schools. Therefore it is essential that collaborative time in schools is focused on capacity building to assure high levels of quality student learning."

—Pam Robbins and Harvey B. Alvy

"Great discoveries and improvements invariably involve the cooperation of many minds. I may be given credit for having blazed the trail but when I look at the subsequent developments I feel the credit is due to others rather than to myself."

—Alexander Graham Bell

"'Networking' [means] 'exchanging information for mutual benefit.'

"'Coordinating' [means] 'exchanging information and altering activities for mutual benefit and to achieve a common purpose.'

"'Cooperation' [means] 'exchanging information, altering activities, and sharing resources for mutual benefit and a common purpose.'

"'Collaboration' [means] 'exchanging information, altering activities, sharing resources, and enhancing the capacity of another for mutual benefit and to achieve a common purpose.'"

—Arthur Himmelman, as quoted
by Kathy Gardner Chadwick

"When teachers share in decision-making, they become committed to the decisions that emerge. They buy into the decision; they feel a sense of ownership; therefore, they are more likely to see that decisions are actually implemented."

—C. H. Weiss, J. Cambone, and A. Wyeth

"What distinguishes leadership from other types of relationships is that, when it works well, it enables people to collaborate in the service of shared visions, values, and missions."

—Lee G. Bolman

CASE STUDY AND REFLECTIVE QUESTIONS

Kathy Bobbitt always wanted to become a teacher. She recalls how, in her early childhood, she used to role-play "teacher" with her younger brothers. "I was so taken with the power I thought my teachers had. Since I was reticent, even withdrawn at times, and lacking confidence, such role playing gave me the 'umpf' I needed." Kathy's reasons for becoming a teacher had matured since her youthful days. As a caring and sensitive individual, Kathy knew her calling was to help others achieve their goals. She had learned so much from her teachers that she wanted to "give something back to others." "There is nothing like teaching . . . helping someone else achieve her personal goals." In the ensuing years Kathy earned several teacher-of-the-year awards and in one year earned the district's coveted "community service award." Well-liked and now quite extroverted, Kathy developed a sterling reputation as a teacher.

After her 11th year of teaching, she decided to enroll in an advanced certificate program leading to state certification as a school administrator. "I love teaching and probably would love doing so for 20 more years. However, I think I want to now serve in a position of 'different' influence." She explained to her partner, Sue, that she felt serving as a principal would allow her to "help so many others." Although she acknowledged the importance of a classroom teacher, she realized that schoolwide, enduring, positive change would not occur unless addressed at the organizational or institutional level. Teacher leadership positions beyond the classroom or grade level were undeveloped in her school district. That's why she decided to become a principal.

One of the primary projects she undertook as part of her leadership program was framing a vision statement or educational platform that would reflect her commitments to educational leadership. She was a fervent believer in collaboration. "Collaboration," she maintained, "is a process whereby educators at different levels of influence work together in systematic, intentional ways in order to effect schoolwide learning for all students." Kathy's vision statement, culled in part below, received noteworthy attention from her professors and eventually from school leaders. Within a short time, she was offered her first principalship, during which time she would try to actualize her vision of collaborative leadership.

In regard to her vision of instructional climate, governance, and leadership, Kathy wrote the following (note that the excerpts below are culled, in part and with permission, from Janice Micali, a student in a leadership program leading to principalship certification):

The realization of student outcomes is inextricably tied to the instructional climate. My vision is of the school as safe harbor or sanctuary in which students, staff, and parents feel safe and nurtured, and in which there is an atmosphere of personal responsibility and mutual respect. The culture of the school would support ***collaboration****, foster reflection, and celebrate accomplishment. Multiple opportunities for celebration of individual and schoolwide success in all areas of achievement would be developed. Student work would be prominently displayed throughout the building, and efforts to acknowledge each student's strengths would be encouraged. Classrooms would be print and material rich, and students would have daily access to technology. A code of appropriate behavior would be developed, agreed upon, and modeled by all. Consequences for inappropriate behavior would be clear and consistently enforced by all members of the school community.*

The school climate would also support professional development that is an outgrowth of self-assessment and reflection, and that supports ***collaboration and collegiality****. All staff members have the capacity for professional growth. My vision is to create a culture that supports teachers in fulfilling this capacity by providing new teacher training, leadership opportunities, meaningful staff development, [and] experience in innovative educational practices and strategies. Opportunities for staff to develop and refine their instruction would be organic, teacher-directed, and sustained throughout the year. Flexible programming would provide time for teachers to participate in weekly study groups to examine student work and teacher practice in the context of the standards. Each study group would follow specific protocols and be facilitated by a peer coach.* ***Collaboration*** *would be encouraged at every turn. Teachers would participate in weekly peer observations, and classrooms would serve as demonstration sites for specific organizational and instructional practices. Structured opportunities for daily interaction among staff around instructional issues and ongoing reflection and* ***collaboration*** *among colleagues about student work and outcomes would replace one-day trainings and workshops. Ample professional resources would be housed in the professional library so as to support all aspects of the professional development program.*

Time and funding for teachers to participate in professional conferences would be provided, with the expectation that they would turnkey this training. In this way, a cadre of in-house specialists would be developed to build schoolwide capacity and foster the development of a community of learners. Parents would also have ample opportunities to develop the capacity to be partners in the children's education. My vision is to create a ***collaborative*** *culture.*

*Essential to the realization of my educational vision is a model of governance and leadership that supports, in the words of Hargreaves and Dawe (1989), "****true collaboration****" and a sense of personal accountability to a set of guiding principles, and that includes and encourages multiple perspectives. In this model, the principal would be responsible for providing the time and the structure for students, staff, parents, and other school community members to openly participate in some aspect of the governance process. This would require identifying specific issues and constituencies and creating multiple governance forums, as well as ensuring that* ***all stakeholders are involved*** *at some point as appropriate. This includes not only teachers, parents, and students, but custodial and cafeteria staff, health providers, and members of community-based organizations. The principal would also create an environment that fosters open,* ***collaborative*** *dialogue among the various stakeholders and that provides training in the new paradigm of the* ***shared decision-making*** *process. In this environment, the goals of the school would be developed* ***collaboratively*** *with student achievement as the focus, and the progress toward the goals would be assessed through a process of ongoing reflection and* ***collaboration****. The specific structure of the assessment component would be developed by the school community and would incorporate multiple assessment models, both formal and informal. Responsibility for student achievement would be shared by all stakeholders, and finger pointing and blaming would be replaced by an atmosphere of* ***collegiality and collaboration*** *in which each member of the school community would take responsibility for the successes and the failures.*

As the leader in this school culture, I would model the values, beliefs, and behavior I sought to engender. My leadership style would be proactive, flexible, ***collegial****, and reflective. I would be genuine in my commitment to a* ***collaborative*** *approach to leadership and [would] sustain a constant focus on the fundamental belief that student achievement must drive all aspects of the educational process. I would maintain an open-door policy, seeking input from members of the school community and participating in the* *reflective process. I would actively work to secure the resources needed to support the instructional process and to develop and sustain a supportive and open relationship with the district and the community. I would lead by example, and demonstrate those qualities of integrity, focus, and mutual respect that are fundamental to my vision of a school community. I would share in both the joys of our successes and in the struggles of our setbacks. I would be coach, facilitator, and exemplar, sustaining the vision and holding the guiding principles continually in the forefront of all our endeavors.*

Although all this seems idealistic, I truly believe in my vision and will work my utmost to achieve my goals. I will not be thwarted. Not because I am overly confident or—heaven forbid—arrogant, but because when a principal ***involves others*** *in leading, sustained commitment to the school is assured. I believe in the power of the many. I believe that teachers will work earnestly and* ***collaboratively*** *when encouraged and acknowledged for doing so.*

Reflective Questions

1. Why is Kathy so committed to collaborative leadership?
2. How realistic is her vision statement?
3. Given information about Kathy, what specific strategies might she employ to facilitate collaborative leadership?
4. How does your vision of the work of a principal differ from Kathy's statement?
5. What obstacles is she likely to encounter, and how might she "thwart" or overcome them?

As mentioned in the Introduction, the first chapter that follows builds upon the preceding information by highlighting some "best practices" for helping you create the team spirit so crucial for collaborative leadership. These ideas are not meant to be exhaustive of the topic, but merely a means to encourage thinking about what it means to serve collaboratively.

Chapter Two

Best Practices in Team Building

"Although team building is a common expression and is well understood, the concept of team learning is relatively new. Traditional team building focuses on improving individual team members' skills as a means for working with each other. It leads to improved communication, contributes to more efficient and effective task performance, and builds stronger relationships among the members. Team learning is different. . . . It is about getting a team to function as a whole rather than as a collection of individuals. Team learning begins with a high level of self-knowledge and progresses toward developing understanding of and aligning with other team members. It encompasses goals of team building but extends far beyond."

—Joyce Kaser, Susan Mundry,
Katherine E. Stiles, and Susan Loucks-Horsley

As the quote indicates, this chapter could be retitled "Best Practices in Team Learning." In fact, this chapter will indeed follow the lead of the quotation by beginning with best strategies (practices) that encourage self-knowledge. Then, strategies will be offered to develop an "understanding of and aligning with other team members." Team building in this vein must be viewed as a means to enhance and improve the *learning* of all members of the school community.

Later in the chapter, we will begin the first of a series of team-learning strategies, but let's first address what is meant by the term *team*. Certainly, the word *team* conjures up a sports image. A baseball team, for instance, is a group of talented individuals who work together, supported and guided by a manager, for a common end or purpose. Individuals play specific roles. Individual achievements are coordinated in a way that benefits the whole. A well-organized and smoothly functioning team produces the best results. We in schools do not very often see ourselves as part of a team. Teachers work too often in isolation of other teachers. Opportunities to join outside the classroom are sporadic and unplanned. Individual teachers develop independent professional relationships with the principal. A team or group effort to accomplish specific goals is often unacknowledged. Some principals see their work as inspiring individuals to help students succeed. It is the rare principal who believes and works to develop and enhance a team spirit wherein many teachers work together for a common purpose. Efforts, in this context, are coordinated with opportunities for groups of teachers to meet on a regular basis in order to strategize and problem-solve. Group visioning is encouraged as well.

A Horatio Alger ethic of working on one's own is no longer viable. According to Biech (2001), "Teamwork is not natural for most of us. Why is that? Most of us were brought up to do the best we could as individuals" (p. 12). Teamwork, however, is essential. Working with others for the common good is necessary. Principals must disabuse others who hold fast to the notion that "I can do better myself." The talents of the many should be tapped into and channeled positively for the greater good. A diverse group of committed leaders at many quarters is needed to promote high achievement for all students. Schooling today, as we mentioned earlier, is too complex to allow for a "go-it-alone" attitude and work ethic.

> *"Most leaders want to accomplish goals that matter, inspire others to join them in working toward those goals, and leave a legacy after they have gone."*
>
> —Andy Hargreaves and Dean Fink

But why work on a team? Biech (2001, p.2) identifies 12 advantages of working on teams that are relevant:

1. More input leads to better ideas and decisions.
2. Higher quality output.
3. Involvement of everyone in the process.
4. Increased ownership and buy-in by members.
5. Higher likelihood of implementation of new ideas.
6. Widens the circle of communication.
7. Shared information means increased learning.
8. Increased understanding of other people's perspectives.
9. Increased opportunity to draw on individual strengths.
10. Ability to compensate for individual weaknesses.
11. Provides a sense of security.
12. Develops personal relationships.

Clearly, these advantages support the goals and objectives of collaborative leadership within a school. To present a balanced perspective, Biech (2001, p. 4) also identifies 12 disadvantages to working in teams:

1. Requires more time.
2. Can lead to many meetings.
3. Often difficult to schedule mutual time.
4. Requires individuals to give more of themselves.
5. May take longer to make a decision.
6. May be used as an excuse for a lack of individual performance.
7. Personality conflicts are magnified.
8. Disagreements can cause strained relationships.
9. Potential for subgroups to form.
10. Teams can become exclusive rather than inclusive.
11. May lead to unclear roles.
12. "Group think" can limit innovation.

Although we certainly should remain wary of these disadvantages, effective collaborative leaders build support mechanisms to avoid or limit possible negative consequences. For instance, a principal might do the following for each disadvantage noted above:

1. Provide in-school time for committees to work.
2. Limit the number of meetings by ensuring each meeting has an approved agenda with a well-organized chairperson conducting the session.
3. Use creative scheduling.
4. Reward individuals for "giving of themselves" (e.g., personal accolades, public acknowledgments).
5. True, but establish a time table.
6. Teamwork not does abrogate the principal from supervision and evaluation.
7. Inevitable, but good interpersonal and conflict-resolution skills can mitigate difficulties.
8. Team building (learning) is particularly valuable here. Also, the principal should personally intercede by meeting with each person.
9. True, but these groups may be channeled positively toward accomplishing a related task.
10. Building teams with term limits and regularly scheduled elections can avoid this problem.
11. The chairperson or principal must charge team members with explicit instructions that are monitored monthly, formally and informally.
12. Bringing in new members or guests from time to time can stimulate development of fresh ideas.

Team building, then, is an important prerequisite to establishing a collaborative learning organization.

Reflective Questions

1. What is your reaction to the notion of "team learning"?
2. What other advantages and disadvantages can you list for team building?
3. Consider leaders you have known and know, and describe how they approach team building. What do they do that stands out in your mind? Would you call them collaborative leaders? Explain why or why not.

The boxed material below summarizes the teaching ideas highlighted in this chapter. The list is not exhaustive but is merely meant to highlight some key concepts and ideas that successful collaborative leaders should know about as they go about influencing others to work together. Brief reflective activities follow each major concept to provoke thought on ways to implement or further understand each idea.

What You Should Know About Team Building

- **Leading With Passion, Vision Building, and Teamwork**—We review Clifton's seven requirements for effective leadership that impact on our work as collaborative leaders, as cited by Bruckner (2004).
- **Ten Characteristics of Successful Teams**—We review Biech's (2001) 10 characteristics of effective teams.
- **Assessing Your Leadership Style**—We review Glanz's (2002) leadership style analysis in order to gain self-knowledge, an important prerequisite to team building and learning.
- **Draw a Pig**—This is an interesting ice-breaking activity useful in team building.
- **The 25 Questions Team-Development Exercise**—An exercise to enhance team members' relationships with one another, to encourage team discussion about work-related topics, and to clarify assumptions about team participation.
- **Team Effectiveness Critique**—Assess how well the team is functioning.

1. LEADING WITH PASSION, VISION BUILDING, AND TEAMWORK

A collaborative leader who is committed to building a team spirit is enthusiastic. Enthusiastic principals are passionate for their work. When one is passionate, one usually enjoys the job, particularly when working with others. Enthusiasm is not a skill, however. It is not something that one can develop after taking a course. It is, rather, a state of mind. It is the awareness that "the glass is half full, not half empty." It is a way of looking at the world, at the school as an organization. It is a belief that one can indeed make a difference. It is a belief that a diverse group of educators can band together for the greater good. An enthusiastic principal views the world and difficult situations, not through rose-colored glasses, but with an abiding sense of the positive, believing that possibilities exist where others see hopelessness. Enthusiasm is not generated merely in situations of crises but rather in the way in which a principal goes about his or her work on a daily basis.

> *"A leader is a person who can rally support to move forward."*
>
> —Donald Clifton

Passion, however, is not enough. Associate Superintendent Marsha Bruckner (2004), relying on the work of Donald Clifton, outlines seven requirements for effective leadership. Her views become relevant as we discuss collaborative leadership. As we highlight these seven aspects of effective leadership, keep in mind your work as collaborative leader:

1. *Tend your vision.* Be involved in frequent visioning and looking forward. Clifton said that true leaders "put dates and events in the calendars of others." In other words, they influence the priorities that others plan for. He hypothesized that a leader should think about the future at least 15–20 times a day.

2. *Turn vision into goals.* Without goals, a vision can languish. A leader has to go beyond merely envisioning the future and take action to make the vision a reality.

3. *Mentor others toward leadership.* Effective leaders know that they cannot succeed alone. Mentoring others ensures that the

leader's vision does not die if he or she departs from the project or organization.

4. *Exhibit self-knowledge.* Knowing one's own strength is vital to effective leadership.

5. *Conceptualize.* A leader needs to know her theory or "map" and continually test it. Leaders need to muse, to go off alone and think. In our fast-paced environment, taking time to reflect is regarded as a luxury; we need to acknowledge that it is a necessity.

6. *Share values.* Others in an organization need to see consistency in a leader's actions. Our colleagues need to know we will always value and believe in certain things.

7. *Build a constituency.* Always work to build a team and to give others ownership in the team. Clifton suggested that every day must be a campaign day if we are to succeed at reaching our vision (cited in Bruckner, 2004, p. 2).

> *"Collegiality is the most important element in the success of and commitment to school improvement."*
>
> —William Cunningham and Donn Gresso

Bruckner (2004) makes the connection to team building as follows: "Along with believing in a vision, a leader must believe in the power of teamwork" (p. 2). Rallying others around a vision and maintaining an optimistic and enthusiastic persona are effective ways of building teams willing to commit to school improvement.

Reflective Question

1. How do passion, visioning, and teaming relate to your work as principal? Provide a case in point.

2. TEN CHARACTERISTICS OF SUCCESSFUL TEAMS

Scenario: Juan Rodriguez, a newly appointed principal in Region 20 in an urban school district in the Northeast, grapples with a senior faculty unwilling to try new teaching strategies and approaches. Their former principal retired after 25 years. His traditional methods were tolerated by the faculty because he rarely, if ever, entered their classrooms. As "captain of the ship," he remained in the main office handling administrative matters. Rodriguez's new style of collaboration was unwelcome and viewed with suspicion. One teacher, Martha Klein, confided to Principal Rodriguez that the former principal had once tried to mandate collaboration since he was expected by the (then) district office to develop a leadership team. "It was a fiasco," explained Mrs. Klein. She continued, "There were no clear goals established. The people he selected didn't even want to be there. No one knew what was expected of them. Some even thought that the principal didn't even care; in fact, he wanted the venture to fail, some thought." Concluding her comments, she reported that "arguments were frequent. Within a short period of time, committee members wouldn't even speak to one another. Chaos and conflicts reigned supreme." "No wonder," thought Principal Rodriguez to himself, "there's so much reluctance and resistance to collaboration now."

> *"A team is a group of people who are mutually dependent on one another to achieve a common goal."*
>
> —Elaine Biech

Although Principal Rodriguez has an uphill struggle, he will likely succeed by reaching out to a few teachers willing to innovate. Success breeds success. Within a two-year period, his passion and vision for teamwork will find fruition. He will not make the same mistakes, however, that his predecessor made. He will keep in mind Biech's (2001) research on effective teams. According to Biech, successful teams possess 10 similar characteristics:

1. *Clear goals.* Everyone is on the same page. All team members know where they are heading. They have a purpose articulated and understood by all members. The team has a collaboratively developed goal. Consequently, confusion is minimized, and meetings are more purposeful.

2. *Defined roles.* Each team member has a task or responsibility. Accountability is ensured.

3. *Open and clear communication.* Communication skills are taught and practiced.

4. *Effective decision making.* Team members work diligently to achieve consensus. Although alternate forms of decision making

exist (e.g., majority rule, expert decisions, authority rule with discussion), team members prefer consensus making.

5. *Balanced participation.* Considering the previous four steps, balanced participation ensures that everyone contributes. Everyone is kept in the proverbial loop.

6. *Valued diversity.* Diversity of ideas is encouraged and expected.

7. *Managed conflict.* Conflict is almost inevitable. In fact, principals and team members should expect it. Although unruly conflict can lead to frustration and worse, managed conflict is possible, and problems are resolvable.

Biech (2001, p. 21) identifies several benefits of "healthy conflict" as follows:

- Conflict forces a team to find productive ways to communicate differences, seek common goals, and gain consensus.
- Conflict encourages a team to look at all points of view, then adopt the best ideas from each.
- Conflict increases creativity by forcing the team to look beyond current assumptions and parameters.
- Conflict increases the quality of team decisions. If team members are allowed to disagree, they are more likely to look for solutions that meet everyone's objectives. Thus, the final solution will most likely be better than any of the original solutions that were offered.
- Conflict allows team members to express their emotions, preventing feelings about unresolved issues from becoming obstacles to the team's progress.
- Managed conflict encourages participation. When team members feel they can openly and constructively disagree, they are more likely to participate in the discussion. On the other hand, if conflict is discouraged, they withdraw.

8. *Positive atmosphere.* Meetings are conducted in an atmosphere of trustworthiness and respect for all.

9. *Cooperative relationships.* Cooperation is fostered through the use of positive reinforcements, constructive feedback, self-evaluation, and recognition of achievements.

10. *Participative leadership.* Participants are encouraged to lead in ways that make them feel comfortable. According to Biech (2001), "Leaders share the responsibility and the glory, are supportive and fair, create a climate of trust and openness, and are good coaches and teachers" (p. 25).

Biech (2001) concludes her discussion by highlighting a big advantage of the team approach to leadership, explaining that "a high performing team can accomplish more together than all the individuals can apart" (p. 25).

Reflective Question

1. How might you implement Biech's 10 characteristics in your school? Assess the degree to which you manage each of the 10 characteristics.

3. ASSESSING YOUR LEADERSHIP STYLE

In the Introduction, we stated that one of the fundamental assumptions of this book and series is that educational leadership can emerge for all quarters of the school organization. In order for collaboration to work and be sustained, leadership by many is necessary. Although a principal can initiate collaboration, the participation of many others is required to sustain meaningful and ongoing partnerships for the benefit of students and the school at large. Further, in a chapter devoted to team building, this notion of distributed leadership is relevant. In fact, all members on a team are leaders. This notion may vie with your traditional conception of leadership as reserved in the hands of one or a few individuals. Such a view of leadership is not only antiquated but not conducive to building enduring learning and commitment to the complex enterprise we today call schooling. Leadership, then, is conceived in this work as a shared responsibility of all participants.

This conception of leadership as people of different qualities or personalities working together toward a shared goal necessitates individuals who know "their strengths and weaknesses, their personality preferences, what drives and motivates them, and how they have an impact on others" (Moxley, 2000, p. 112). This part of the chapter focuses on self-knowledge as an important attribute of those engaged in activities of team leadership. The information here will encourage and assist you in identifying an appropriate and well-matched style of leadership. The information presented here is brief. Readers interested in further insights may want to refer to the Best Resources section (Resource E) later in the book.

One parenthetical note is in order before we begin to explain this theory of leadership styles. As explained earlier, team building necessitates self-understanding in order for each member to function as a valued, contributing team member. Many assessments can be used to attain self-knowledge. A plethora of learning style inventories, for instance, exist that readers can take to gain self-knowledge. The Myers-Briggs tool (http://www.hiresuccess.com/myers-briggs.htm?source=overture&OVRAW=%22Myers-Briggs%22&OVKEY=myers%20briggs&OVMTC=standard) is quite popular and research based. Another one is the Kolb approach, found at http://pss.uvm.edu/pss162/learning_styles.html. Many other assessment instruments may be applicable. You are encouraged to take any additional instrument, because the greater knowledge you have of your own abilities, interests, and inclinations, the better leader and team member you will become.

* * * * * * * * * * * * * * * *

Warren Bennis (1989), authority on leadership, once said that the point "is not to become a leader. The point is to become yourself, to use yourself completely—all your skills, gifts, and qualities—in order to make your vision manifest. You must withhold nothing. You must, in sum, become the person you started out to be, and enjoy the process of becoming" (pp. 111–112). This statement summarizes well the point here. Good leaders know themselves and use their talents to improve schools (see, e.g., Buckingham & Clifton, 2001). Although you are who you are, you can, in Bennis's view, "become" *more* yourself—you can grow and improve and become an even better leader.

Another leadership authority, Moxley (2000) explained that self-knowledge is an

> important attribute of those who engage in the activities of leadership. Our identity helps determine how we understand and practice leadership and engage in relationships that are integral to it. Individuals engaged in the practice of leadership must know their strengths and weaknesses, their personality preferences, what drives and motivates them, and how they have an impact on others. (p. 112)

These are the messages we will amplify below.

Self-awareness, the ability to form and understand identity, is critical to good leadership. The qualities we possess shape us. They identify who we are and what we can do. Understanding our qualities is the core to understanding ourselves. Daresh (1996) posited that "knowing oneself" is essential, perhaps even more so than knowing "how to do the job." Aristotle made the point even more strongly: "The unexamined life is not worth living."

Leadership is about people of different qualities working together toward a shared goal. Leadership does not focus solely on the capacity of one person, usually called the "boss." Although a "boss" is the staple of most organizations, other individuals with different characteristics or qualities are equally essential. Leadership in this sense is a broad, inclusive activity in which combinations of quality groups work together toward a common goal.

Working together toward a common goal presupposes that we have identified the right individual for a particular task or situation. Good leaders ask, "Do we need an architect? An innovator? A stabilizer? A campaigner? A healer? A designer? A sustainer?" How we match the leadership quality (style, character, personality) of an individual to the needs of the situation is critical for effective leadership.

> *"In a collaborative school, all staff members engage in the study of learning and those practices that facilitate the learning process."*
>
> —Pam Robbins and Harvey B. Alvy

The ideas here are premised on the following:

- *Everyone can lead* in some way, to some degree, in a given situation, at some time.
- *All leaders are not the same.* Leadership styles, personalities, or traits vary greatly.
- *No one way of leading is better than another.* Each leader is talented in a different way.
- *Effective leadership depends on the context.* Matching the right leader to a particular situation is most important.
- *Leadership is relational.* It emerges and develops from a social situation that is nurturing, allowing for trial and error and continuous learning.
- *Effective organizations need all types of leaders.* Different leaders positioned strategically throughout a school or district can contribute greatly to organizational effectiveness.
- *Leadership is central to the work of teams and critical in any collaborative effort.* Identifying leadership talents in all team members is essential for team success, for collaboration is most effective when each person understands his or her own role.

Assessing Your Leadership Style: The Survey

The ideas in this section are drawn from Glanz (2002, with permission from the Association for Curriculum and Development; based on Null, 1996) but have been extended and refined based on ensuing research. Take the following survey, meant to provide feedback to explore your leadership proclivities.

Directions for Completing the Survey

1. Below, you will find 56 statements.

2. Next to each number, write True (T) or False (F) for each statement.

3. If a statement describes the way you think you are, for the most part, then indicate True (T); if the statement does not describe you, indicate False (F). You MUST write True (T) or

False (F). Some statements may be difficult to classify, but please indicate just one answer.

4. Your responses are anonymous. The surveys cannot accurately assess these attributes without your forthright responses to the various statements. You need not share your responses with anyone. Obviously, the accuracy of these instruments is dependent both on the truthfulness of your responses and the degree to which you are aware that you possess or lack a certain attribute.

5. Using the chart below, circle numbers that you recorded as true.

6. After you complete the survey by recording your responses in the chart below, follow the directions to tabulate and interpret the results.

Answer Sheet

(True or False to each statement in each survey)

Am I an AAS?	*Am I a CAS?*	*Am I an AS?*	*Am I a DAS?*	*Am I a DS?*	*Am I a DAG?*	*Am I an AAG?*
1	2	3	4	5	6	7
14	13	12	11	10	9	8
16	15	18	17	20	19	21
30	29	22	24	23	28	25
31	39	32	27	26	41	33
35	40	36	37	34	47	42
38	44	46	48	45	49	43
56	55	50	54	51	53	52

The Surveys

1. I feel I'm good at supervising a small group of people, and I enjoy doing so.

2. When I'm in a new situation, such as a new job setting or relationship, I spend a lot of time comparing it to analogous situations I've been in previously.

3. I believe that respect for authority is one of the cornerstones of good character.

4. I enjoy thinking about large issues, such as how society is organized politically.

5. I get asked for help a lot, and I have a hard time saying no.

6. Ever since childhood, I've always seemed to want more out of life than my peers did.

7. When I first enter a new environment, such as a workplace or a school, I make it a point to become acquainted with as many people as possible.

8. I rarely seek quiet.

9. I can work harder than most people, and I enjoy doing so.

10. When I meet a person I'll give that individual the benefit of the doubt; in other words, I'll like someone until he or she gives me a reason not to.

11. The idea of a lifelong and exclusive intimate partner doesn't seem desirable or realistic for me.

12. A lifelong relationship with a romantic partner is one of my goals.

13. I can sometimes work creatively at full throttle for hours on end and not notice the passage of time. I'll periodically go through extremely low-energy periods during which I have to remind myself that it's only a phase.

14. I believe that divorce is to be strongly avoided whenever possible.

15. I'll periodically go through extremely low-energy periods during which I have to remind myself that it's only a phase.

16. When it comes to spending and saving habits, I take pride in being more thrifty and less foolish than most people.

17. Being alone does not scare me; in fact, I do some of my best thinking when I'm alone.

18. My extended family is the most important part of my social life.

19. I spend much less time than others do on what I consider pointless leisure pursuits, such as TV and movie watching; novel reading; and card, computer, or board game playing.

20. I procrastinate a lot.

21. My vacations are always highly structured; several days of just sitting in one place and vegetating would drive me crazy.

22. Directing a big job and supervising a lot of subordinates is my idea of a headache.

23. People usually like me.

24. I find myself getting frustrated because most people's world-view is so limited.

25. Networking as a career and life tool is something that comes naturally to me.

26. I'm happiest interacting with people and aiding them in some way.

27. I have a drive to express my ideas and influence the thinking of others.

28. I find myself getting frustrated because most people operate at a slower pace than I do.

29. I find myself getting frustrated because most people are not on my mental wavelength.

30. I generally believe that if individuals behave outside the norms of society, they should be prepared to pay the price.

31. My home is more organized and cleaner than most people's in my neighborhood.

32. Holding one job for decades would be OK with me if the conditions were good and the boss was nice.

33. When tackling a problem or task, I'm usually less defeatist than others.

34. It sometimes takes an outside force to get me motivated, because I tend to be satisfied with what I have.

35. I enjoy the feeling of my life going along at an even pace like a well-oiled machine; too many stops and starts and ups and downs would really upset me.

36. Trying to lengthen your life by eating the "right" foods doesn't make much sense to me because when your time's up, your time's up.

37. I have no trouble getting people to listen to me and grasp what I'm saying.

38. I understand that detail work is what ultimately gets a job done, and I have the gumption and know-how to tackle details.

39. Working by myself is no problem; in fact, I prefer it.

40. At times, ideas just "come to me," and if I can't put them down then and there—on paper, canvas, and so on—I'll be uncomfortable until I can.

41. I could never be really happy working for someone else.

42. I like associating with influential people and am not intimidated by them.

43. I'm happiest moving and doing, as opposed to sitting and thinking.

44. Throughout my life there's been a pattern of people calling me one or more of the following: "temperamental," "moody," "sad," "flighty," "different," and I never really felt like I was "one of the boys" or "one of the girls."

45. People tell me I have a great sense of humor.

46. I believe that blood is thicker than water and that it's more important to be loyal to your relatives than to your friends.

47. I don't have much time or patience for long family gatherings, such as a whole afternoon spent celebrating Thanksgiving.

48. The makeup of my social circle is constantly changing.

49. Managing a big job and having subordinates carry out the detail work is my ideal kind of endeavor.

50. I prefer to work at a job a set number of hours each day and then have the rest of the 24 hours for relaxation.

51. I'm good at smoothing over others' conflicts and helping to mediate them.

52. I thrive on setting goals for myself and then figuring out how to reach them; I can't imagine just drifting through life without a plan.

53. I'm more intelligent than most people, and others almost always recognize this.

54. I can't fathom the idea of holding one job for decades.

55. I find competition distasteful.

56. I would never dress in a flashy, bohemian, or otherwise attention-getting way.

Directions for Tabulating the Results

1. For each category (e.g., "Am I an AAS?") count the number of True (T) responses in that column. Record your fraction score on the chart below. Note that the numerator represents the number of "True" responses and the denominator represents the total number of questions on the survey (which will always equal 8, because each survey has eight questions). For example, if you recorded "T" for seven out of the eight items in the first column, "Am I an AAS," then your fraction will be 7/8.

2. Complete the table below by referring to your responses on the Answer Sheet on page 29.

	Am I an AAS?	*Am I a CAS?*	*Am I an AS?*	*Am I a DAS?*	*Am I a DS?*	*Am I a DAG?*	*Am I an AAG?*
T's/8							

Interpreting the Results

1. Your Natural Leadership Quality is found under the category in which you scored the highest number of "True" responses. For example, if you scored 8/8 for "Am I a DS?" then your quality is "DS." Perhaps no category earned an 8/8, but one category (e.g., "Am I a CAS?") had 7/8, whereas all the others were lower (6/8 and less). In that case, your quality is "CAS."

2. Although most respondents will find their highest score in one category, some respondents may have two or more categories with equally high scores. For example, you may have scored an 8/8 in two categories. If so, then your quality is represented by those two categories. If no category received an 8/8, locate the next highest score. For example, your highest score may be 5/8, and three categories may have earned that score. If this is the case, then your quality is represented by those three categories.

3. In the chart below, circle the quality or qualities that scored the highest number of "True" responses.

   AAS CAS AS DAS DS DAG AAG

4. The meaning of these results will become clear as you read on. Please note the following caution: No one assessment can accurately assess one's inclinations or abilities. These surveys are meant to stimulate interest, thought, and discussion for purposes of exploring leadership in schools. Examine the results in light of the theories and ideas expressed in this book and make your own determination of their relevance and applicability to you personally and to your work in schools.

Assessing Your Leadership Style: What It Means

Each of us manifests a particular quality or style. We feel most comfortable when we exercise discretion to use and live by that style. The qualities are as follows:

- **Dynamic Aggressives (DAG)** represent the smallest percentage of the population
- **Dynamic Assertives (DAS)** represent the change agents, reformers, or iconoclasts
- **Dynamic Supportives (DS)** represent the nurturing helpers
- **Adaptive Aggressives (AAG)** represent individuals who aggressively pursue a goal
- **Adaptive Assertives (AAS)** represent excellent organizers
- **Adaptive Supportives (AS)** represent most of the people one ever meets
- **Creative Assertives (CAS)** represent visionary and artistic individuals

We will next examine each of these qualities by defining its essential characteristics and how each quality manifests itself in different people.

We have natural qualities and attributes that make us unique and that drive or motivate us. How we react in a particular situation or crisis is determined by these "natural" qualities. While many of us possess a constellation of attributes in differing amounts, we fall back on that dominant attribute or personality trait that comes most "naturally" to us in times of crisis or need.

A principal, for example, may have been hired in a school that has been beset by "warring" factions to articulate a schoolwide vision in which all vested interests can reach consensus. Yet, this principal, although managerially very competent, may not have the "natural" dynamic and charismatic qualities to bridge disparate viewpoints and factions. We must consider the match between the "natural quality" and the task that needs to be accomplished. Not everyone has the same potential to bring the aforementioned school to consensus. The principal, while competent and able to do many important things, may not be a good match for the needs of this school at this time.

What can we say about these attributes or qualities in general? On one end of the spectrum, an individual may demonstrate charisma that can naturally influence or attract other people. On the other end of the quality spectrum are people who feel no need to stand out in any way. Rather, their expertise is in their ability to adapt well to any situation and to work diligently to accomplish their objectives. Each of these qualities, and the ones in between, has its own resonance, strengths, and weaknesses.

The Primary Quality Types

In terms of natural leadership quality, three main types of people exist: the Dynamics, the Adaptives, and the Creatives (see Figure 2.1). Dynamic individuals possess a charismatic quality, a personal magnetism that enables them to inspire and lead others. Dynamics have an ability to see the larger picture, can articulate a vision for the future, and have a strong sense of ego (think of Margaret Thatcher, Bill Clinton, or Nelson Mandela as examples of this primary quality type). Adaptives, in contrast, are not charismatic, nor are they looking to change the broad scope of situations; their sense of ego is much less than that of a dynamic. Creatives have a different personal rhythm, awareness, and sensitivity that allow them to perceive the world differently and more imaginatively than Dynamics or Adaptives.

These three main quality types are distinct from one another. If you've met a dynamic individual, you are not likely to forget her or him. They take center stage and possess the personal magnetism that attracts others to them and their ideas. These qualities occur "naturally." An Adaptive or Creative, in contrast, may "act" or appear charismatic at times, but this characteristic doesn't come naturally. The characteristics of each quality occur naturally and without contrivance.

The Secondary Quality Types

Within the broad types, three further divisions exist. Some people are characteristically aggressive, some assertive, and some supportive (see Figure 2.2).

The Aggressives have a driving, forceful quality and tend to lead or want to dominate others. These are dominating, take-charge people. Have you ever served on a committee and noticed one individual who immediately engages the group forcefully? These individuals have a need to be at center stage.

In contrast, some people, the Assertives, feel quite comfortable sitting back and listening. Although these people are not driven to take charge immediately, they are confident and will be willing to put forth their strong views on matters at the right moment.

Supportive individuals are not the natural leaders, and they are not usually the most eloquent speakers. They act best in their supportive roles. They are basically nurturing, happy to help, and truly concerned about the welfare of others.

Putting Them Together to Form Seven Quality Types

All of us, of course, possess a degree of each quality. We all can demonstrate, at times, creativity, adaptiveness, and even dynamism. Again, the point is that each of us has a "predominant" natural quality. When we operate in our quality type, we feel most comfortable and productive. It is "who we really are" when the curtains are drawn and we are alone.

As noted above, the primary qualities combine with the secondary qualities to form seven distinct quality types (see Figure 2.3). For a complete discussion of each of the seven quality types, see Glanz (2002). Research data confirm the principles below:

- **Most people exhibit a tendency toward one quality over another.** In cases where individuals exhibit strong tendencies in more than one area, the qualities are likely complementary.

- **We exhibit a particular quality as a natural consequence of who we are.** In other words, these qualities manifest themselves uniquely and naturally. The particular quality comes easily and naturally to us. For instance, I may act dynamically, but if I am not naturally dynamic I may come off as just plain pushy. Each person should be allowed to express her- or himself in a specific quality. For example, parents who both are Creative Assertives may have a child who naturally displays Adaptive Assertive tendencies. If these parents "coerce" the child to behave in a certain way based on their own qualities, the child will likely feel upset and dysfunctional. An Adaptive Assertive child can never display the natural creativeness that Creative Assertives manifest.

• **Each quality operates on a continuum between high (up) and low (down).** A Dynamic Aggressive, for instance, may work to her or his potential and thereby achieve much good for an organization. If, however, the person is operating at the low end, she or he may exhibit some rather obnoxious and unethical behaviors and thus may not contribute very much to the organization. In fact, operating at the low end of the Dynamic Aggressive quality may cause the most harm to an organization.

Reflective Questions

1. Assess your personal leadership style. What did you learn or confirm about yourself?
2. How can these leadership styles help build effective learning teams?
3. Have your views of leadership changed in any way? Why or why not?
4. How might you use this self-knowledge survey in your efforts in team building and collaborative leadership in general?

Significance of Leadership Styles to Collaborative Leadership

You understand that one's leadership style may influence how one responds to a particular crisis or situation. You are aware of your own style, which includes leadership strengths and limitations. You may be prepared to identify leadership qualities in others matched to the needs of a specific situation or context. For instance, as principal, you wouldn't place a Dynamic Aggressive or even an Adaptive Supportive teacher in a role that requires meticulous planning, detailed organizational skills, or creative problem-solving abilities. You realize each leader is unique and brings an array of qualities to a particular situation or responsibility.

"A collaborative culture builds leadership and helps develop a learning environment in a school."

—L. Joseph Matthews and Gary M. Crow

Figure 2.1 Primary Quality Types

• Dynamics	Would others characterize you as highly charismatic?
• Adaptives	Would others realize that although you are neither charismatic nor creative, you adapt well to varied situations?
• Creatives	Would others acknowledge your imaginative or artistic ability?

Figure 2.2 Secondary Quality Types

• Aggressives	Would others characterize you as highly opinionated, or even contentious?
• Assertives	Would others realize that you are a secure and confident person?
• Supportives	Would others acknowledge your encouraging and affable nature?

Figure 2.3 Seven Quality Types

	D	A	C
AG	DAG (Dynamic Aggressive)	AAG (Adaptive Aggressive)	
AS	DAS (Dynamic Assertive)	AAS (Adaptive Assertive)	CAS (Creative Assertive)
S	DS (Dynamic Supportive)	AS (Adaptive Supportive)	

Collaborative leadership is enhanced by understanding how each person contributes to the school mission. Collaboration requires the participation of many, but you understand that not all people can contribute in the same way. You realize the contributions and possible limitations of each style. The descriptions below serve merely as one example, but they are illustrative:

- **Dynamic Aggressives** are not particularly interested, at least initially, in collaborating with others just for collaboration's sake. They enjoy getting involved in visioning big ideas on their own, but they are willing, later on, to excite and work with others to actualize their hopes and goals.

- **Dynamic Assertives** rally others toward school reform and institutional change. They collaborate with others only when they feel that others will share their particular views of change. They are astute enough to realize that they cannot "go it alone."

- **Dynamic Supportives** are most willing to share and learn with and from others. They are natural collaborative leaders. They believe in collaboration because they are very people oriented. Sometimes, though, they have to be encouraged to take a greater decision-making leadership position.

- **Adaptive Aggressives** will collaborate with others, but only on their own terms and with a specific end in mind. Collaboration for them occurs conditionally, not out of genuine desire to work with people, as might a Dynamic Supportive. Adaptive Aggressives usually have ulterior motives or agendas. Still, they can work with others skillfully to get the job done.

- **Adaptive Assertives** may work with others on projects because they understand that the more sets of eyes, the better the end product. Yet, they may stubbornly wish to "do it on their own" because they feel most others may not share their enthusiasm, persistence, conviction, and even compulsion.

- **Adaptive Supportives** are natural followers and are very willing to join in with others toward a common goal. They may not be willing, initially, to take the lead on a project, but they will serve in any way they can.

- **Creative Assertives** enjoy collaboration when such efforts are innovative and stimulating. They enjoy collaborating and offering their creative talents for the greater good. They may need the assistance of, say, an Adaptive Assertive to structure their participation or presentation.

Collaboration isn't easy. Smart principals see and capitalize on the unique talents of people in and around their organization. When you tap into each person's talent and bring people together, you will find that collaboration succeeds. Collaboration occurs best when a mix of styles works together on a large project. For more specific ventures, such as creative brainstorming sessions, you might want to rely more on a particular style (i.e., Creative Assertive).

4. DRAW A PIG

The next several best practices in the remainder of the chapter focus on a variety of team-building strategies this author has found effective. Please note that there are so many more team-building and ice-breaking activities that are useful. Refer to Resource E for additional ideas and techniques.

This first activity is drawn from http://gs.fanshawec.ca/ppoole/edcn/WEEK%203/Stuffweek3/Teachertrainingtruecolors.htm.

Step #1: Have participants take out a blank piece of 8 1/2-inch × 11-inch paper and ask them to "draw a pig."

Step #2: When people are finished drawing, read the following:

If you drew your pig:

- Toward the top of the paper—You are positive and optimistic.
- Toward the middle—You're a realist.
- Toward the bottom—You're pessimistic.
- Facing left—You believe in tradition, are friendly, and remember dates (especially birthdays).
- Facing forward—You are direct, enjoy playing the devil's advocate, and neither fear nor avoid discussions.
- Facing right—You are innovative and active, don't have strong sense of family, and don't remember dates.

- With many details—You are analytical, cautious, distrustful.
- With few details—You are emotional and naive, care little for details, and are a risk taker.
- With all four legs visible—You are secure, stubborn, and stick to ideals.
- With fewer than four legs visible—You are insecure, living through a period of major change.
- The size of ears indicates how good of a listener you are—the bigger the better.
- The length of tail indicates quality of life—more is better.

Step #3: After folks giggle, lead a discussion on the meaning of the results. Ask, "Did you learn anything about yourself?" "Did you learn anything about a fellow team member?" (Personal account: One fellow told the group, "This activity doesn't really relate to me, but it hit the nail on the head about Jim . . . he really is an optimist." This led to a deeper discussion of how each of the aforementioned descriptions or qualities manifest themselves in different members of the committee.)

I will not reproduce here other icebreakers, such as the common one that asks participants to solve a set of riddles, usually about 20 boxed items to a page. Most of you have seen or used them before. They are excellent, though, to generate laughs, curiosity, and interest. See the Best Resources section (Resource E) for suggestions.

Reflective Question

1. How might you use the activity above?

5. THE TWENTY-FIVE QUESTIONS TEAM-DEVELOPMENT EXERCISE

Goals

- To enhance the team members' relationships with one another.
- To stimulate a team discussion about work-related topics.
- To clarify assumptions that the team members make about one another.

Group Size: All members of an ongoing team.

Time Required: Approximately one and one-half hours.

Materials: A copy of the Twenty-Five Questions Form for each team member.

Process:

1. The facilitator introduces the goals of the activity and briefly discusses the importance of being open in relationships with coworkers and of obtaining feedback on one's work style. (Five minutes.)

2. The facilitator distributes copies of the Twenty-Five Questions Form, explains the ground rules, and elicits and answers questions to ensure that each team member understands the procedure. (Five minutes.)

3. The facilitator asks the team members to volunteer to initiate questions. (The team members may need to be encouraged to confront one another. For example, each member may be asked to read the list of questions silently, to select one question, and to look around the circle and choose one person to become the focus of that question. Then the facilitator may solicit a volunteer to ask a question; after each question has been asked and answered, the facilitator may need to encourage others to volunteer. Also, some direction from the facilitator may be required for questioners to answer their own queries.)

4. The facilitator interrupts the question-and-answer procedure after about 30 minutes to assist the team members in discussing how the activity is progressing. Questions such as the following may be useful:

   - Who questions whom?
   - How open are we being?
   - What risks are present in this activity?
   - To what degree is trust being generated?
   - What are we learning about ourselves?
   - What are we learning about one another?

- Whom might you want to do this with privately?
- How might we improve the activity in the next round? (Fifteen minutes.)

5. The procedure is resumed, and the team members are urged to note any change that can be attributed to the processing intervention of the previous step.

6. After about 20 minutes, the procedure is stopped. The facilitator encourages the team members to respond to the question "If we were to quit right now and never do this again, what question would you regret not having asked someone?"

7. The entire activity is critiqued by the team members, and its implications for the team's continued development are discussed. The team members make plans to use the same questions in a follow-up session to be held in a few months.

Variations

- The team members may be paired in the initial phase to work through as many questions as they can during the time allotted. Then in the second round the risk taking may be increased by forming pairs on the basis of a variety of criteria (for example, leader and follower, people who know each other least well, and people who think that they are different from each other).

- The question form may be supplemented with items suggested by the team members.

- An entirely different question form may be generated from items suggested by the team members. For example, the team members may have a discussion of what they would need to talk about in order to increase openness and trust in their interpersonal relations. The resulting items may be duplicated later for use in a subsequent session.

- Each team member may be asked to write a name or names at the end of each of the 25 questions when the list is read for the first time. This approach may heighten the volunteering.

- In an extended session (two to three hours), the process may be interrupted several times so that the team members can rate themselves and the team on honesty and risk taking (see the continua that follow). Subsequently, the two scales are displayed on newsprint, and the members record their ratings independently on blank paper.

Dishonest, evasive		ME			Completely honest, open
0	1	2	3	4	5
		THE TEAM			

Playing it safe		ME			Taking many risks
0	1	2	3	4	5
		THE TEAM			

Twenty-Five Questions Form

Ground Rules: The list of questions below is designed to stimulate team discussion of work-related topics. The following ground rules should govern this discussion:

1. Take turns asking questions, either to specific individuals or to the team as a whole.
2. You must be willing to answer any question that you ask.
3. Any member may decline to answer any question that someone else asks.
4. Work with the person who is answering to make certain that effective two-way understanding takes place.
5. All answers remain confidential within the team.

Questions (may be asked in any order):

1. How do you feel about yourself in your present job?
2. What do you see as the next step in your career development?
3. What personal characteristics do you have that get in the way of your work?

4. What are you doing best right now?
5. What are you trying to accomplish in your work?
6. Where do you see yourself ten years from now?
7. How are you perceiving me?
8. What would you predict to be my assessment of you?
9. What was your first impression of me?
10. How many different kinds of responsibilities do you have?
11. How do you typically behave when a deadline is approaching?
12. What kind of relationship do you want with me?
13. What things do you do best?
14. What factors in your job situation impede your goal?
15. Which team member are you having the most difficulty with right now? (What is that person doing? What is your reaction?)
16. To whom are you closest in your work situation?
17. Where would you locate yourself on a ten-point scale of commitment to the goals of this team (1 = low, 10 = high)?
18. What part are you playing in this team?
19. How do you want to receive feedback?
20. What do you think I am up to?
21. What puzzles you about me?
22. How are you feeling right now?
23. What issue do you think we must face together?
24. What do you see going on in the team right now?
25. What personal-growth efforts are you making?

SOURCE: Biech, *The Pfeiffer Book of Successful Team-Building Tools.* © 2001. Reprinted with permission of John Wiley & Sons, Inc.

> **Reflective Question**
>
> 1. How might you use the activity above?

6. TEAM EFFECTIVENESS CRITIQUE

How well is your team or committee functioning? Assessment along the way is important to overall success. Administer the "Team Effectiveness Critique" (copied with permission on the next page) as a way of assessing how your team is functioning. Break into groups or conduct a whole-team discussion about findings. Brainstorm strategies for improving deficiencies, if any.

Instructions: Indicate on the following scales your assessment of your team and the way it functions by circling the number on each scale that you feel is most descriptive of your team.

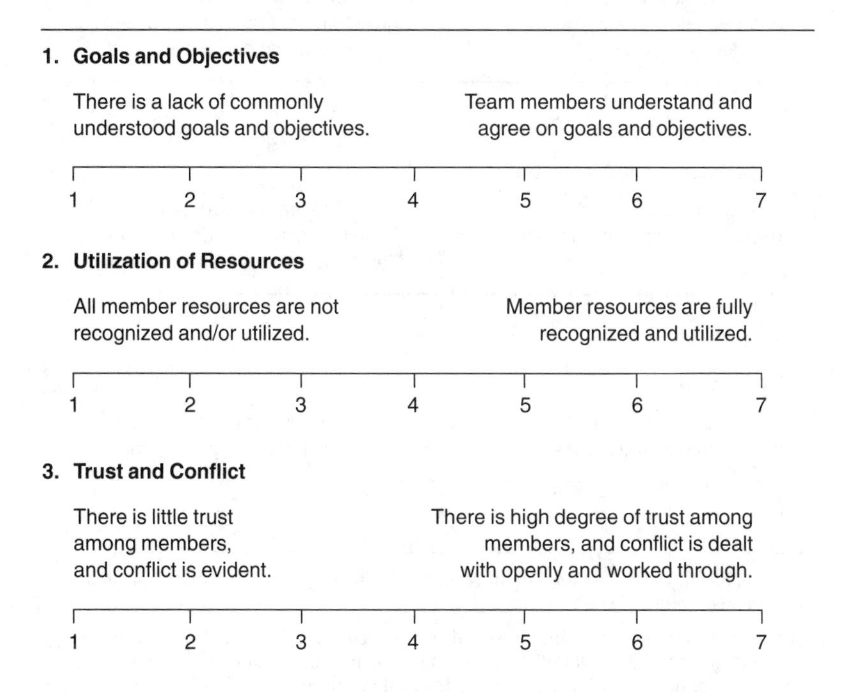

1. Goals and Objectives

There is a lack of commonly understood goals and objectives. — Team members understand and agree on goals and objectives.

1 2 3 4 5 6 7

2. Utilization of Resources

All member resources are not recognized and/or utilized. — Member resources are fully recognized and utilized.

1 2 3 4 5 6 7

3. Trust and Conflict

There is little trust among members, and conflict is evident. — There is high degree of trust among members, and conflict is dealt with openly and worked through.

1 2 3 4 5 6 7

4. Leadership

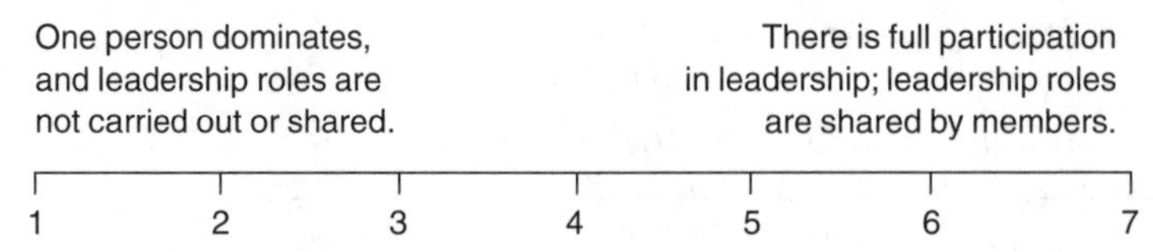

5. Control and Procedures

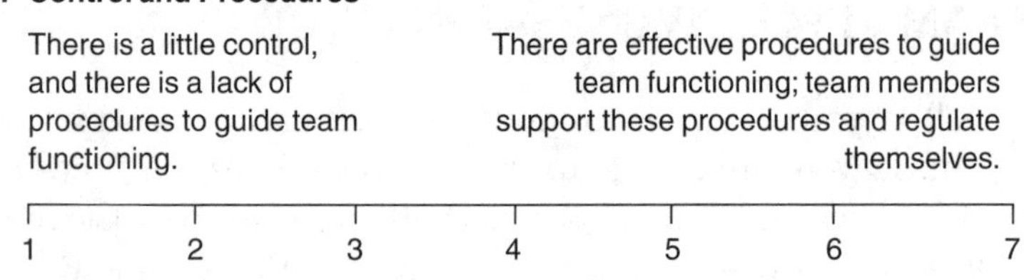

6. Interpersonal Communications

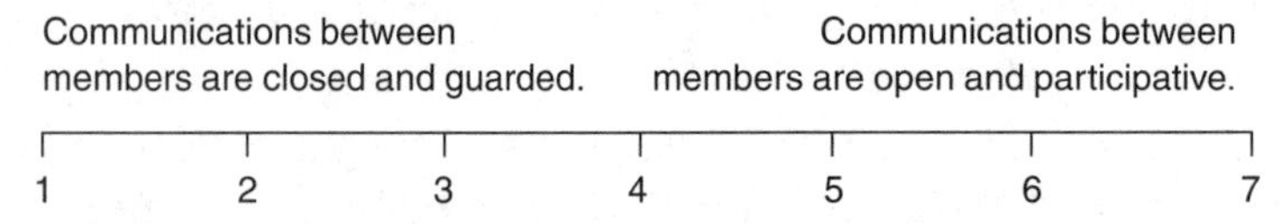

7. Problem Solving/Decision Making

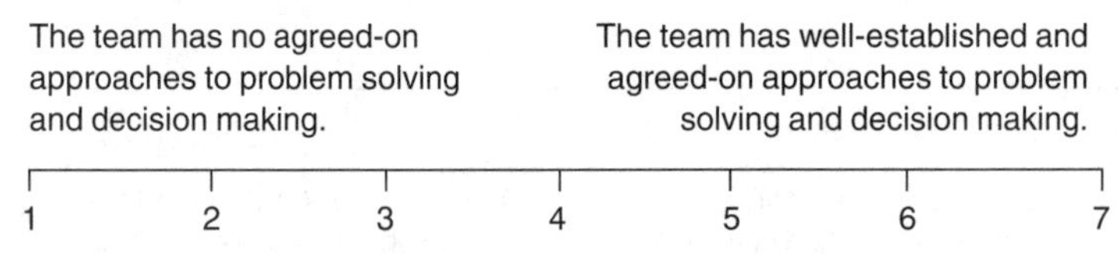

8. Experimentation/Creativity

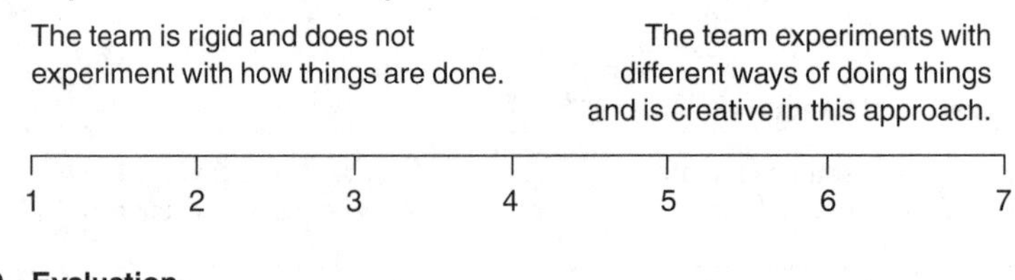

9. Evaluation

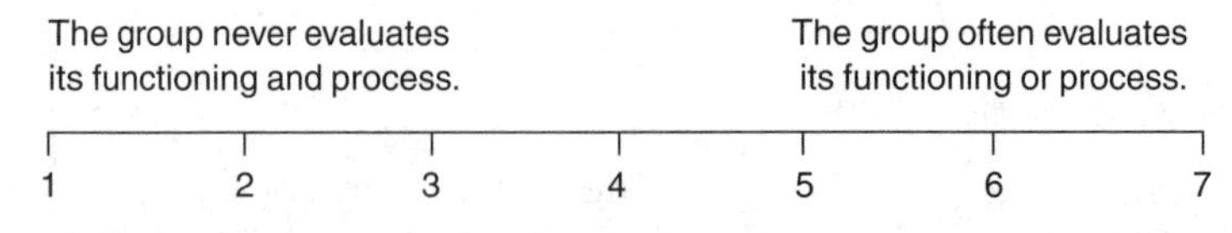

SOURCE: Biech, *The Pfeiffer Book of Successful Team-Building Tools.* © 2001. Reprinted with permission of John Wiley & Sons, Inc.

Reflective Question

1. Assess your personal degree of humility. In what instances were you humble, or less so?

CONCLUSION

Too many of us do not take the time to team-build. We assume that adults already possess collaborative skills or that they can learn as they go. It is not wise to do without this critical element in team building because, as was stated at the outset of the chapter, as team members engage in these activities, they learn as well. These learning experiences are the foundation upon which future collaborative relationships are built. Once a faculty, for instance, is tainted because of poor interrelationships, it becomes very difficult, if not impossible, to get them back on board toward achieving some common schoolwide goal. Team building is an invaluable opportunity for learning. All educators must learn and grow together. This is an important principle in collaborative leadership.

> *"The reward of a successful collaboration is a thing that cannot be produced by either of the parties working alone."*
>
> —Harlan Ellison

This chapter has highlighted seven requirements for effective collaborative leadership, 10 characteristics of effective teams, assessment of one's leadership style, an icebreaker activity, an exercise to build and learn together, and finally an evaluative instrument to gauge how well a team is progressing.

The key issue in team building is how best to make these efforts an everyday leadership practice. Some advice might serve as a guide before we move on to the next chapter. Consider each decision you make and ask yourself, "What value is there in soliciting input from others?" Post a note on your desk or bulletin board as a reminder to involve others. This suggestion may seem trite or superficial, but too often we get caught up in crises and may overlook the benefit of involving others. Learn patience, because not all decisions have to be made on the spot. Sometimes this may be difficult for Adaptive Aggressives or Adaptive Assertives. Nonetheless, remain vigilant. Get out of your office and interact with others on a consistent basis. Invite their input. Build team spirit by talking about how the school is really a group of professionals committed to a unified goal. Offer positive reinforcement to all participants on every possible occasion. If you really believe in team building, then you'll take these and other suggestions to mind and put them into action.

The next chapter focuses on participating on action research teams, which is so critical for schoolwide learning and improvement.

Chapter Three

Action Research as Best Practice for Collaboration

"Although action research is not a quick fix for all school problems, it represents a process that . . . can focus the brain-power of the entire instructional staff on maximizing learning."

—James E. McLean

What You Should Know About Action Research

- **Action Research for Collaboration and More**—Principals utilize action research work to build strong relationships among faculty/administrators and in order to promote student achievement.
- **Benefits of Action Research**—Once we realize the benefits of action research, we may be very willing to implement such work, even though it may be somewhat time-consuming.
- **Steps in Action Research**—Learn the four easy steps that you can apply quite easily.
- **Three Forms of Action Research**—Action research can be used in three ways.
- **Action Research in Action**—Two case studies are provided to show how it works.
- **Guidelines for Implementing Action Research**—Some practical suggestions for principals are offered.

ACTION RESEARCH FOR COLLABORATION AND MORE

By now, I hope you are convinced of the importance, value, and usefulness of collaboration in your work as principal. You have articulated a vision of collaborative activity for your school and have gathered like-minded individuals who have practiced team building. You are now ready to put all that effort into practice. Action research is an ideal, currently in vogue, and research-based educational strategy that can rally faculty around a pressing issue in need of exploration. Action research is disciplined inquiry used to reflect upon and solve practical problems that we may face. Faculty members, along with school administrators, can collaborate to solve urgent instructional or curricular matters that address a particular grade level or the school as a whole. Further, effective principals use action research as a meaningful way to reflect upon issues affecting the school. One of the chief by-products of using action research as a planned schoolwide method of inquiry is the formation of strong interpersonal bonds among members who participate. Intentioned, well-meaning collaboration will do that. The process of meeting, exploring, collecting data, analyzing and interpreting them, and drawing plans for action is uplifting, exciting, and potentially beneficial to student learning as well. Action research in this chapter is addressed as a prime example of collaboration at its best. Parenthetically, however, please note that in this short volume devoted to collaboration, action research is treated as a process by which interested educators collaborate around central and mutual concerns. Specifics regarding carrying out research (e.g., data collection methods, data analyses including statistical procedures and qualitative assessments) are best learned by consulting other works devoted exclusively to carrying out action research (see Resource E, "Best Resources").

As the quotation at the outset of this chapter indicates, action research as a collaborative process can bring together thoughtful and committed educators to strategize in order to maximize student learning, the ultimate purpose for encouraging collaboration. Principals, as instructional and collaborative leaders, are responsible, first and foremost, to promote best teaching practice (Zepeda, 2003). Good principals continually engage teachers in instructional dialogue and reflective practices so that they are best equipped to improve the academic performance of all their students. As such principals, you are aware of the varied instructional strategies that aim, directly or indirectly, to improve student achievement.

One of the neglected areas or instruments for instructional improvement is the practice of action research. Once thought of as only a tool to collect data for teacher personal and professional development, action research today is employed by principals as cutting-edge practice that encourages teachers, as thoughtful collaborative professionals, to reflect, refine, and improve teaching. Action research, then, becomes an integral component in any instructional supervision program.

Action research as instructional supervision, however, is a relatively recent phenomenon. Although more and more principals view action research as a meaningful way to involve teachers in instructional dialogue for the purpose of improving teaching and learning, it has not always been so (see, e.g., Glanz, 2003; in press). The field of supervision has moved away from noninstructional approaches towards more collaborative, participatory, and reflective practices aimed at improving instruction (Sullivan & Glanz, 2005). Action research is one strategy among others that reflect this move.

Some Examples of Action Research Yielding Collaboration and Stronger Culture

1. A school is beset by high teacher turnover. You're the newly appointed principal. You were able to hire 14 new teachers of varying levels of prior teaching experience. One half of your teaching faculty is new. You rally interested faculty members around a student problem that has bothered teachers in this inner-city high school for years. By introducing a schoolwide action research project aimed to find best ways to reduce high rates of student tardiness, you engage faculty in collaborative forums. The process, you know, is even more important than the eventual strategies developed by the committee. Such collaborative efforts around a mutual bothersome concern build camaraderie and trust.
2. A school wishing to build a stronger professional development program for school faculty reaches out to a local college for

support. You meet with the chair of the education department to develop a plan to involve college professors with expertise in literacy, learning styles, and differentiated instruction. You collaborate with the education department to collect some data on how well this effort is received among school faculty.

Reflective Question

1. What are the potential benefits of using action research? (See section that follows.)

BENEFITS OF ACTION RESEARCH

Although some educators think that research is impractical, irrelevant, and simply not feasible for practitioners given the exigencies and pressures of working in a school, research, properly used, can have immeasurable benefits:

- Creates a systemwide mind-set for school improvement—a professional problem-solving ethos.
- Enhances decision making—greater feelings of competence in solving problems and making instructional decisions. In other words, action research provides for an intelligent way of making decisions.
- Promotes reflection and self-assessment.
- Instills a commitment to continuous improvement.
- Creates a more positive school climate in which teaching and learning are foremost concerns.
- Impacts directly on practice.
- Empowers those who participate in the process. Educational leaders who undertake action research may no longer, for instance, uncritically accept theories, innovations, and programs at face value.
- Reinforces the impact of "true collaboration."

Considering these benefits, the time spent is worth the effort.

STEPS IN ACTION RESEARCH

Although the purpose here is not to provide a "how-to" approach to undertake action research (refer to Resource E, "Best Resources"), knowledge of the four easy steps will give you a good sense of what is involved. Four guiding steps are as follows:

1. Select a Focus

Includes three steps:

(a) Know what the team or committee wants to investigate.

(b) Develop some questions about the area they've chosen.

(c) Establish a plan to answer these questions.

Come to an agreement on what aspect of the school program they would like to study. Ask, "What are we concerned about?" and "Why are we concerned?" Identify what is known and what needs to be known about this program or practice. Ask, "What do we know about this program?" and "What information should be known in order to improve the program?" Identify specific aspects of the program that might need scrutiny, such as:

Student Outcomes: for example, achievement, attitudes

Curriculum: for example, effectiveness of instructional materials, alignment with state content standards

Instruction: for example, teaching strategies, use of technology

School Climate: for example, teacher morale, relationships between teachers and supervisors

Parental Involvement: for example, participation on committees, attendance at school events

As the team focuses on a specific concern or problem, they need to begin to pose some questions that will serve to guide their research. If, for instance, low levels of parental involvement are a concern in the school, they might ask: "How can we document these low levels of parent involvement?" "What impact do these low levels of participation have on students' completion of science projects?" "Will increased levels of involvement yield higher student achievement levels?" and "How might parental involvement in school affairs be increased?"

Developing these guiding questions will eventually lead to specifying research questions or hypotheses. Selecting a focus also includes developing a research design (see Glanz, 2003; Mills, 2002).

2. Collect Data

Once the team has narrowed their focus (that is, have a specific area of concern, have developed some research questions, and know how they plan on answering them), they are now ready to gather information to answer their research questions. Let's say they're investigating the new science program adopted by the district. They've posed some research questions about achievement levels and students' attitudes toward science. They can now begin to collect data that will provide evidence for the effectiveness of this program in terms of achievement and attitudes. They may administer teacher-made and standardized tests, conduct surveys and interviews, and examine portfolios.

Reflective Questions

1. What other kinds of evidence could they collect to help them understand the impact of this new science program?
2. How would they collect such evidence?

Quite often, action researchers collect data but do not organize them so that they can be shared with others. Raw data that just "sit around" in someone's file drawer are useless. Collected data must be transformed so that they can be used. Data that are counted, displayed, and organized by classroom, grade level, and school, for example, can then be used appropriately during the data analysis and interpretive phases. In order to present action research in the most concise and usable way possible, data organization is required.

3. Analyze and Interpret Data

Once team members have collected relevant data, they need to begin the process of analysis and interpretation in order to arrive at some decision. Data analysis and interpretation of results are essential (Glanz, 2003; Mills, 2002).

4. Take Action

Finally, they've reached the stage at which a decision must be made. They've answered their research questions about the effectiveness of the new science program. At this point, three possibilities exist:

(a) Continue the science program as originally established.

(b) Disband the program.

(c) Modify the program in some way(s).

Action research is cyclical. The process doesn't necessarily have to stop here. Information gained from previous research may open new avenues of research. That's why action research is ongoing. In the role of "educational leader as action researcher" (a.k.a. principal), you're continually involved in assessing

Figure 3.1 Steps in Action Research

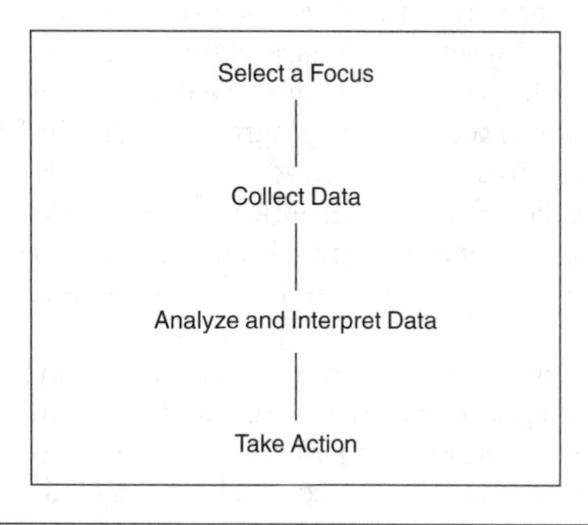

Figure 3.2 Three Forms of Action Research

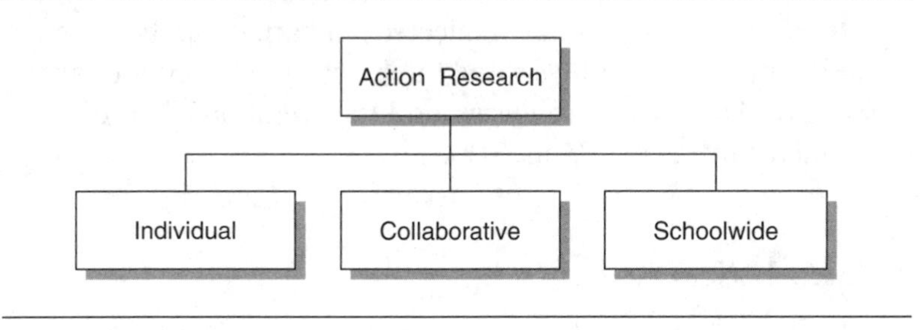

> *"The self-renewing school or district provides colleagueship directly within and across all spheres."*
>
> —Bruce Joyce, James Wolf, and Emily Calhoun

instruction and seeking ways of improving your school. Action research affords you the opportunity and tools necessary to accomplish these lofty goals. Collaborating with and involving others make the whole effort so worthwhile.

THREE FORMS OF ACTION RESEARCH

Three forms of action research allow educators to investigate areas of concern in their classrooms and schools: individual, collaborative, and schoolwide (see Figure 3.2; Calhoun, 1993). Individual teachers and principals may conduct a research project that focuses on a specific class, program, or activity. The educator may define an area of investigation and then seek a solution or may simply collect data to determine a course of action. All action research projects, indeed, begin with an individual educator who has the necessary knowledge, skills, and desire to carry out such an enterprise.

Collaborative action research is a *form* of action research that is taken on by a group or team of individuals that can, for instance, focus on one classroom or several classrooms. A collaborative action research team may also conduct a districtwide investigation

(Oja & Smulyan, 1989). Schoolwide action research, a third form of action research, is undertaken by a community of practitioners including teachers, parents, students, and administrators to address schoolwide issues and solve common problems (see, e.g., Calhoun, 1994; Calhoun, Allen, Halliburton, & Jones, 1996; Sagor, 1992; Stringer, 1996).

The distinction between collaborative and schoolwide research may be subtle, or even arbitrary. Certainly, a school faculty committee that involves parents and students, for instance, is collaborative in nature. Action research projects are more likely to be encouraged and supported by principals who have experienced firsthand the benefits of this type of research on a small scale. Outside consultants can be hired to assist, if necessary.

ACTION RESEARCH IN ACTION

First popularized in the 1940s by Kurt Lewin (Adelman, 1993), action research has since served as a problem-solving strategy for improving the school organization (Corey, 1953; Lewin, 1948), as a process of individual reflection on practice (Elliott, 1991), as a process to support staff development (Oja & Smulyan, 1989), as a collaborative process to support teachers' professional development (Sagor, 1992), and as a strategy to guide site-based school improvement by educators within a school building who collaborate as a team (Glickman, 1998).

While few educators, historically, ever described the role of principals beyond overseeing or administering the action research process, thus enabling teachers to successfully complete a particular project, Hilda Taba (Taba & Noel, 1957) was among the first educators to envision the principal as integral to the process. Taba explained that principals needed expertise in action research not only to facilitate teachers' work, but to "act as a research technician, devising, adapting, and borrowing research techniques as needed" (Taba & Noel, p. 50). More recently, action research, building on past efforts to make supervision more collaborative and reflective, is viewed as a supervisory approach that not only engages teachers in reflection about their teaching, but encourages teachers to examine pedagogical practices that directly influence student achievement (Calhoun, 2002; Danielson, 2002; Marzano, Pickering, & Pollock, 2001). Although originally developed primarily for the professional development of teachers, action research has recently gained favor among principals as a way of improving schools by focusing on reflective, collaborative practice for instructional improvement.

The two case studies that follow will demonstrate more specifically action research "in action." The first case study, about one teacher, is drawn from a larger study that examined alternatives to supervision (see Sullivan & Glanz, 2000). Doris Harrington is a tenured math teacher at Northern Valley Regional High School, a school that comprises 1,100 students. Having taught in the school for 18 years, Doris is excited about the new program that Principal Bert Ammerman spearheaded to enhance professional development and instructional improvement. "I think it's neat that we now have a system in place in which we feel empowered. I mean, having an option, a choice in determining my professional development is certainly new and much appreciated."

Doris selects an "action research" plan as a part of the supervisory program that teachers, supervisors, and administrators *collaboratively* developed. "I've read so much about action research and am so excited that others now appreciate how important it is to provide time for teachers to reflect about what we do every day in the classroom." Doris's observations confirm many educators who maintain that encouraging effective teaching is one of the most important responsibilities of instructional supervisors (Schon, 1988).

Familiarizing herself with the literature on action research (Glanz, 2003; Mills, 2002), Doris reviews the four basic steps: (a) selecting a focus for study, (b) collecting data, (c) analyzing and interpreting the data, and (d) taking action. She wonders about her classroom. "What has been successful? How do I know these strategies are successful? What needs improvement? What mistakes have I made? In what ways can I improve my instructional program?" Most important, "What instructional strategies that I use work best with my students in a given subject or topic?" In *collaborative* conversations with her assistant principal, Jim McDonnell, Doris frames her project.

She wonders whether or not the time and energies expended on cooperative learning activities are worth the effort. Although familiar with the extensive research on the subject, Doris decides to compare her fourth-period math class with her sixth-period class in terms of how cooperative learning strategies will affect student achievement and attitudes toward problem solving in mathematics. She chooses these two classes because they are somewhat equivalent in mathematical problem-solving ability. She selects a nonequivalent control group design commonly associated with ex post facto research, because the study involves the use of intact classes.

She randomly assigns "cooperative learning" as the primary instructional strategy to be used with the period 4 class, while the other class will work on mathematical problem solving through the traditional textbook method. After six weeks of implementing this plan, she administers a posttest math exam and discovers, after applying a *t*-test statistic, that the group exposed to cooperative learning attained significantly higher mathematical problem-solving scores than the group taught math traditionally. Doris keeps an anecdotal record throughout the research project and also administers an attitude questionnaire to ascertain how students felt about learning math using cooperative learning groups as compared to learning math in the more traditional format.

Based on her findings, Doris decides to incorporate cooperative learning procedures with all her classes. In consultation with Jim McDonnell, she develops a plan to continue assessments throughout the year. Jim asks Doris to present her findings at both grade and faculty conferences. As a result of her efforts in association with the principal and assistant principal, Doris encourages other teachers in the school to join in a *collaborative* effort to undertake a schoolwide action research project.

Doris's enthusiasm for action research was emphatic:

> Employing action research engenders greater feelings of competence in solving problems and making instructional decisions. In the past I never really thought about the efficacy of my teaching methods to any great extent. The time spent in this project directly impacts on my classroom practice. I'm

> much more skeptical of what really works and am certainly more reflective about what I do. Action research should, I believe, be an integral part of any instructional improvement effort. No one has to convince you to change an instructional strategy. Once you gather and analyze your own data, you'll be in a position to make your own judgments about what should or should not be done. Action research empowers teachers!

Also illustrative of "Action Research in Action" is the case of The International High School (IHS), a multicultural alternative educational environment for recent arrivals to the United States, serving students with varying degrees of limited English proficiency (Nadelstern, Price, & Listhaus, 2000). The school's mission is to enable each student to develop the linguistic, cognitive, and cultural skills necessary for success in high school, college, and beyond.

IHS is a learning community in which professional development is not a separate initiative but, rather, is built into everything that is done. The faculty and the student body are organized into six interdisciplinary teams. On each team, four teachers (math, science, English, and social studies teachers) and a support services coordinator are jointly responsible for a heterogeneous group of about 75 9th through 12th graders. The faculty works with the same group of students for a full year, providing a complete academic program organized around themes such as "Motion," "Conflict and Resolution," or "The American Dream." Teams also provide affective and academic counseling.

The interdisciplinary teams provide an ideal infrastructure for professional development. Significant decision-making power over curriculum and even supervision is delegated to the teams. Team members engage in action research as not only an alternative to traditional supervision, but more importantly as a means to support faculty professional development and, ultimately, student learning.

In this second case study, we find Maria Rodriguez, Bill Evans, Fred Alvaro, and Martha Cunningham (names and events are fictionalized) working together on a team. Integral to professional development at IHS is reflection. Time is structured into the workweek for planned reflection. Team members are free to brainstorm ideas on a wide variety of topics. Any team member can raise a problem or concern for group reaction. During one of these "reflective" sessions, Maria was concerned about students' test scores in writing. Other members shared her concern. Statewide examinations in writing had been mandated two years earlier, and the team was concerned that preliminary data indicated students were significantly deficient in this area, especially since little attention had been previously paid to writing under the former administration. Team members met over the summer to decide on a curriculum plan for teaching writing, eschewing prepackaged writing programs all too common in other schools in the city. After much research and in consultation with a prominent local university, the team decided to implement a rather well-known writing program sponsored by the university, although with significant modifications. Infusing writing in all content areas, together with individual and small-group "writing consults," the team set out to make writing a priority in the fall semester. The team decided to field-test the new program with a randomly selected group of students in 10th grade and identified a comparable group of 10th graders not in the program.

Supporting the team, Eric Nadelstern, the principal at the time, provided targeted professional development and encouraged action research strategies to track program success. He encouraged teams to use action research to demonstrate the impact of teaching on student writing achievement. As part of the program, students kept detailed writing portfolios that contained writing samples over time, illustrating writing maturity. Writing assessments were continuously administered. Detailed monitoring of student progress, along with constructive feedback, were hallmarks of the program. After the administration of the statewide writing examination in May of that academic year, team members met to assess the impact of the program on student achievement, student writing motivation, and on the effectiveness of the teaching strategies employed by the teachers.

The following chart summarizes their findings:

Instrument	*Standard*	*Percentage Meeting*	*Conclusion*
Standardized writing achievement test	50% above 50th percentile	65% above 50th percentile (25% improvement over previous year); only 35% of girls scored above norm	Expectation met; examine achievement of girls (interviews, etc.)
Writing portfolios	At least 50% scoring "acceptable" on portfolio rubric	55% scored "acceptable," but only 15% for girls	Expectation met overall, but examine achievement for girls
Monthly teacher-made exams	At least 50% scoring "acceptable" on writing rubric for idea development, sentence structure, and grammar	80% scored acceptable, but significantly less for girls	Expectation met overall, but examine achievement for girls
Student surveys	At least 80% registering satisfaction with new approach to writing	70% approval rating, but only 10% for girls	Expectation not met; further study needed

Team members analyzed the data and conducted a comparative analysis with the control group. The team shared their findings with other teams and charted a course to expand the program and address the reasons why girls did not score as well as boys.

Eric Nadelstern encouraged Maria, Bill, Fred, and Martha to reflect on the process of using action research to monitor student writing progress but also to consider how such research strategies provide evidence of the impact of their teaching on student achievement. During one brainstorming session, the dialogue went something like this:

Fred: I felt kind of empowered using alternate means of assessment to measure student writing progress. Not relying on the standardized test alone was refreshing, even though in this case the state exams reflected our qualitative and quantitative findings.

Martha: I know what you mean. Using research strategies to track student progress helped me greatly to adjust my teaching approaches in the classroom. For instance, after monitoring their progress, I realized what worked and didn't work, and so I made changes.

Bill: Well, that may be true, but it appears we weren't sensitive or attuned to the needs of girls. Having these data alerts us to something we may not have picked up as readily or quickly.

Martha: You're right, Bill. I guess we first have to analyze the data more closely and perhaps collect some more information through group focuses or one-on-one interviews with some of the girls. Then we'll have to differentiate instruction to accommodate their needs and do some more action research to ascertain any improvements. [Bill nods in affirmation, as do the others]

Maria: For me, this action research project provided structure to make sure I—I mean, we—reflected as we proceeded. I'm not sure I would have done so myself.

Fred: Yeah, we acted as a team, participating to solve a common problem.

Martha: Also important is the fact that we were always conscious of the relationship between our teaching practices and the impact they would have on student achievement.

Eric Nadelstern [to himself]: No need to formally observe these teachers . . . action research provided the means to encourage reflection in order to promote instructional improvement and student learning.

Reflective Questions

1. What have you learned about the action research process as a result of the case studies above?
2. How would action research enhance collaborative inquiry in your school?
3. What steps would you take to plan a schoolwide action research project in your school?

GUIDELINES FOR IMPLEMENTING ACTION RESEARCH

Collaboration, participative decision making, and reflective practice are the hallmarks of a viable school improvement program designed to promote teaching and learning. Action research has become an important form of instructional supervision in order to engage teachers in reflective practice about their teaching and as a means to examine factors that aim to promote student achievement. This chapter has highlighted the importance of action research as a means to supportive collaborative leadership. Practical guidelines for implementing action research as instructional improvement are now provided for you as principal.

- *Focus on instructional supervision.* You are very good at compiling reports, engaging with parents, and writing proposals. Although these activities are *important,* remember to attend to *urgent* concerns. Attention to your role as instructional leader is paramount to positively affect teaching and learning. Engage teachers in instructional dialogue and meaningful supervision (not evaluation). Get out of your office and into the classrooms, and save the report writing for down times and after school. Strive to encourage good pedagogy and teaching. Faculty and grade meetings should focus almost exclusively on instructional issues. Avoid quick-fix approaches that presumably guarantee high student achievement. No instructional panaceas exist. Certainly, as principal you feel the increased pressure to raise student achievement. You realize that your job is on the line. Take reasonable and intelligent steps to establish an instructional milieu in your school. Emphasize instruction at every turn, that is, at grade and faculty conferences, in e-mail and memo correspondences, at parent workshops, and so forth.

- *Acknowledge the importance of action research as an important component of an overall instructional supervision program.* Action research, as collaborative and disciplined inquiry, has emerged as a popular way to involve educators in reflective activities about their work. Action research, properly used, can have immeasurable benefits, as mentioned earlier in the chapter.

- *Make time for reflection.* "Reflection? Who has the time?" asks a principal in an inner-city school in Los Angeles. "Certainly, we've learned about 'reflective practice' in graduate courses, but who has much time to really 'reflect' when you're on the job?" complains a principal in a suburban school in Westchester, New York.

Reflective practice is a process by which educational leaders take the time to contemplate and assess the efficacy of programs, products, and personnel in order to make judgments about their appropriateness or effectiveness so that improvements or refinements might be achieved. Research-oriented leaders have a vision that guides their work. As they plan and work to improve their schools, they collect and analyze data to better inform their decisions. Research-oriented leaders are engaged in ongoing self-study in which they assess the needs of their schools, identify problem areas, and develop strategies for becoming more effective.

> *"Collaborative cultures also support risk taking when practitioners engage in rigorous reflection on their practice with a mutual willingness to question underlying assumptions."*
>
> —Robert J. Garmston, Laura E. Lipton, and Kim Kaiser

Instilling habits of reflection, critical inquiry, and training in reflection is not usually part of a principal preparatory program. Principals should submit their own practice to reflective scrutiny by posing some of these questions, among others:

1. What concerns me?
2. Why am I concerned?
3. Can I confirm my perceptions?
4. What mistakes have I made?
5. If I were able to do it again, what would I do differently?
6. What are my current options?
7. What evidence can I collect to confirm my feelings?
8. Who might be willing to share their ideas with me?
9. What have been my successes?
10. How might I replicate these successes?
11. How can I best promote instructional improvement and raise student achievement?
12. In what other ways might I improve my school?

Reflective principals continually think about instruction and ways to promote and enhance student learning by bringing considered people together in the school for purposeful collaboration.

Reflection is the heart of professional practice.

- *Facilitate, don't push.* Instructional supervision at IHS in the second case study above emerged naturally from the supportive school organizational structure. Dividing the faculty into teams encouraged reflection, teamwork, and collegiality. Providing teachers with staff development on action research empowers a faculty to, on their own, implement research strategies to solve or at least better understand practical problems. The principal at the school didn't have to mandate action research as supervision; it emerged as a community of learners was addressing a common concern. A wise principal establishes a conducive environment that encourages reflection. A principal sets the tone for a systemwide focus on student achievement and provides the professional development to support teachers with the resources or tools necessary to improve instruction. Action research as instructional improvement should be facilitated and encouraged.

Reflective Question

1. Which of these suggestions make the most sense? Explain how you might use the advice.

CONCLUSION

Participating in action research projects goes far toward promoting collaboration in a school. The time spent on such committees deepens personal relationships, strengthens school commitments, and plants the seeds for further collaborations. Action research is an invaluable means to promote collaboration, because the types of activities educators participate in are meaningful rather than superficial, purposeful rather than haphazard, and enduring rather than ephemeral. As principal, you can foster collaboration enormously by encouraging educators and others in your school to work on action research initiatives.

This chapter has highlighted the importance and benefits of action research for collaboration. Four steps of action research were reviewed, along with three popular forms that can be practiced in schools. Two case studies were provided to demonstrate how action research might be practically applied in schools. The chapter ended with a few suggestions for implementation.

The next chapter focuses on shared decision making as a best practice to enhance collaboration.

Chapter Four

Best Practices in Shared Decision Making

"Colleagueship does not mean that you need to agree or share the same views. On the contrary, the real power of seeing each other as colleagues comes into play when there are differences of view. It is easy to feel collegial when everyone agrees. When there are significant disagreements, it is more difficult. But the payoff is also much greater. Choosing to view 'adversaries' as 'colleagues with different views' has the greatest benefits."

—Peter M. Senge

"I believe that a theory of the schoolhouse should strive to transform the school into a center of inquiry—a place where professional knowledge is created in use as teachers learn together, solve problems together, and inquire together."

—Thomas J. Sergiovanni

"When teachers accept common goals for students and therefore complement each other's teaching, and when supervisors work with teachers in a manner consistent with

the way teachers are expected to work with students, then—and only then—does the school reach its goals."

—Carl D. Glickman

What You Should Know About Shared Decision Making

- **Encouraging Teacher Leadership**—Interest in teacher leadership is most directly influenced by the work on shared decision making and a vital component of collaborative leadership.
- **Site-Based Management**—Meaningful collaboration cannot occur unless a structure is in place for it to occur.

Public education has received voluminous criticism (Johnson, 1990; Katz, 1987; Sizer, 1984) for being bureaucratic and unresponsive to the needs of teachers, parents, and children. One of the prominent proposals for disenfranchising bureaucracy has been the attempt to more meaningfully involve teachers in decision-making processes (Dunlap & Goldman, 1991). This translated into giving teachers more formal responsibility for setting school policies, thus enhancing democratic governance in schools (Kirby, 1991). Susan Moore Johnson (1990) observed that "although schools have long been under the control of administrators, local districts are increasingly granting teachers more formal responsibility for setting school policies" (p. 337). The argument for greater involvement goes something like this: When teachers participate in decisions about their schools, there will be a significant improvement in their attitudes, which will strengthen their commitment toward their work. It is further hoped that teacher empowerment will translate into better student academic performance (Heck, Larsen, & Marcoulides, 1990). The major premise here is that without a commitment to teacher leadership, shared decision making will not be supported.

Reflective Question

1. Have you seen more of an emphasis on teacher participation and shared decision making in your work in schools? Explain.

1. ENCOURAGING TEACHER LEADERSHIP

Although teachers have participated to varying degrees in curriculum development committees, instructional initiatives, and school improvement projects, their involvement has been haphazard, piecemeal, and limited in duration. The principle of teacher leadership, however, has gained prominence over the past two decades. The current interest in teacher leadership is most directly influenced by the work on shared decision making so prevalent in the literature of the 1980s (Glanz, 1992). Many realize that if significant organizational and especially instructional change is to occur, then teachers must play a more active role (e.g., Spillane, Halverson, & Diamond, 2001). Moreover, since the literature most recently has been replete with the importance of building learning communities (see, e.g., Sullivan & Glanz, 2005), the role teachers are expected to play is significant. Teacher involvement has been seen as especially critical in this era of high-stakes accountability, where the bottom line is high student achievement. Teachers, by all accounts, are the most essential practitioners who directly impact student learning (Cotton, 2003; Leithwood, Seashore Louis, Anderson, & Wahlstrom, 2004).

> *"Teacher leadership is inextricably connected to teacher learning . . . in the course of restructuring, opportunities to collaborate and take initiative are available at every turn."*
>
> —Linda Darling Hammond et al.

York-Barr and Duke (2004) have conducted an extensive review of the literature on teacher leadership. As part of their review, they identify reasons for supporting teacher leadership. They point to the benefits of teacher participation. Encouraging teacher involvement increases the likelihood that schoolwide improvement will occur, because schools today are "too complex for principals to lead alone" (p. 258). Another benefit includes more effective decision making when teachers are given voice to share their perspectives and concerns. York-Barr and Duke explain, "In education, teachers are direct service employees who hold vital knowledge regarding daily operations and interactions with clientele. They are employees whose perspectives can well inform decisions" (p. 258). The fact that teacher involvement enhances "ownership and commitment to organizational goals" is another important benefit (p. 258).

Another reason to encourage teacher leadership centers on the fact that research demonstrates that when teachers are involved in instructional decision making, student learning improves. Given teacher expertise about the teaching and learning process, their leadership is crucial in order to promote instructional improvement. York-Barr and Duke (2004) state, "Teacher expertise is at the foundation of increasing teacher quality and advancements in teaching and learning" (p. 258).

Teacher involvement in school leadership also enhances teachers' own professional development. As Fullan (1995) posited, "Quality learning for all students depends on quality learning for all educators" (p. 5). Citing Barth (2001), York-Barr and Duke (2004) indicate that "only when teachers learn will their students learn" (p. 259). When teachers are actively involved in the school beyond their classroom, they feel a sense of accomplishment and renewal greater than benefits that may accrue within a single classroom. Involving teachers in meaningful and ongoing leadership opportunities goes a long way to recruiting, retaining, motivating, and rewarding the very best teachers.

> *"Teacher cultures, the relationships between teachers and their colleagues, are among the most educationally significant aspects of teachers' lives and work. They provide a vital context for teacher development and for the ways that teachers teach."*
>
> —Andy Hargreaves

Reflective Question

1. Are you committed to teacher leadership? Explain why or why not.

Teacher leadership has been defined in various ways (York-Barr & Duke, 2004); however, Fullan's (1995) conceptualization of teacher leadership seems most comprehensive and sensible. According to Fullan (1995), quality learning depends on the "development of the six interrelated domains of teaching and learning, collegiality, context expertise, continuous learning, change process, and moral purpose" (pp. 5–6). As Figure 4.1 illustrates, educators need us to do the following:

- Understand that teaching is complex and textual (Hare, 1993), that teachers are facilitators of learning (Joyce & Weil, 1999), and that learning occurs when learners construct meaning on their own (Cochran, DeRuiter, & King, 1993).

- Value collegial relationships and participate as active members in a democratic learning community (e.g., Goodlad, 1994; Sergiovanni, 1994).

- Demonstrate a commitment to specific knowledge, understanding, and skills needed for relating to and taking account of parents, communities, businesses, and social agencies (Fullan, 1995) and, as such, appreciate and consider all aspects of cultural diversity among students and community (Nieto, 2003).

- Develop intellectual and emotional habits of critical reflection (reflective analysis) and action about their professional work, realizing that the mark of a professional is exhibited in a sustained effort of self-improvement (Goodlad, 1994).

- Tolerate ambiguity, remain flexible, and be willing to take risks (Ambrose & Cohen, 1997), realizing that in a complex, ever-changing world, educators must not only cope with unpredictable events and trends but must also become agents of change in their own right.

- Believe that teachers make a difference in the lives of all students academically (Cotton, 2003), and that they are driven by a moral purpose that affirms human dignity and a sense of caring for all people (Noddings, 1984, 1986, 1992).

Teaching and Learning

As principal, you realize that the knowledge base for teachers is more varied and complex than ever before. Teachers must draw on multiple teaching strategies to meet a wide range of individual needs. They must understand how diverse, multiethnic students learn and must be skilled in technological applications. They must also possess knowledge of assessment and monitoring techniques to better frame instruction and curriculum.

Teachers need to be prepared for learner-centered schools in which classrooms are humane, interactive, and intellectually

Figure 4.1 Educator (Principal) Development Domains

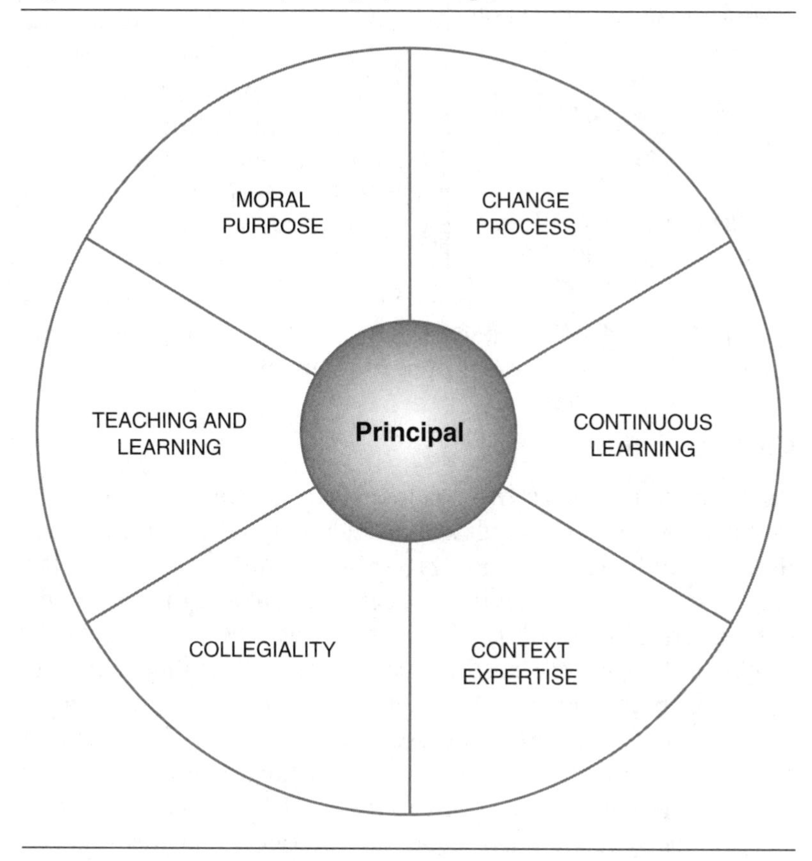

rigorous places. Teachers are concerned with preparing students who themselves are knowledgeable, have requisite academic and social skills, and appreciate the value of lifelong learning. The pursuit of these more challenging approaches to teaching and learning requires strong principal leadership and changes in curricula, school organization, and professional development.

Collegiality

As schools, more and more, move away from traditional forms of school organization, increased demands for reconceptualizing

> *"Successful school administrators recognize the need for innovation, change, and continuous improvement through collaborative efforts to enhance teaching and learning."*
>
> —Frederick C. Wendel, Fred A. Hoke, and Ronald G. Joekel

curriculum and instruction are taking place. Principals now must work closely with other colleagues on instructional, curricular, and administrative matters. In participatory democracies, principals need to be capable of collegial problem solving in the face of complex issues. The collaborative leader understands that the old model of "principal on a white horse" single-handedly solving schools' problems is no longer acceptable, if it ever was.

Context Expertise

Effective principals must demonstrate active involvement in multiple contexts (multicultural and global) and positive interactions in multiple communities (families and agencies). Fullan (1995) states that "leadership and development also means becoming experts in context" (p. 7). This means, according to Fullan (1995), developing expertise in "specific knowledge, understanding, and skills, needed for relating to and taking into account parents, communities, businesses, and social agencies" (p. 7). Becoming experts in context includes "specific strategies for connecting parents to learning, for learning to teach for cultural diversity, and for partnering with other educative agencies and institutions" (Fullan, 1995, p. 7).

Continuous Learning

Reflective practice is a prime vehicle for principal continuous learning. Principals realize the importance of reflective practice in refining their unique knowledge, skills, and dispositions. Principals are aware of the importance of continuous learning not only to stay abreast of the latest developments in the field but also to continually seek self-improvement.

Change Process

Principals certainly need knowledge and skills for understanding and adapting to the dynamics of change. More specifically, principals must know how to initiate change and how to manage change as it naturally occurs within and without the school organization. They must realize that the process of change, which is chaotic and unpredictable, is a natural state of affairs.

Moral Purpose

Society, for many, is in a state of moral crisis. Maintaining high ideals and commitment is an important professional responsibility of principals. If principals are to develop a strong sense of ethics, they must be able to "appreciate the moral-ethical implications of multiple perspectives on complex issues, and to creatively synthesize these perspectives into viable solutions" (Ambrose & Cohen, 1997, p. 21). Principals as collaborative leaders who deal most fundamentally with values must maintain a firm moral grounding.

Reflective Question

1. React to Fullan's conception of teacher leadership. How do his views intersect with your own?

Having reviewed several benefits of teacher leadership and providing a conceptualized view of teacher leadership that is comprehensive, yet specific, via Fullan's (1995) work, let's now examine four conceptions of leadership that relate to teacher involvement. These four ways of conceiving teacher leadership are premised on a notion that leadership is distributed within a school and not vested in a single individual. Hierarchical blockages are removed, communication is enhanced, the focus is on learning, and organizational effectiveness is a priority. According to Duke (1994), "leadership . . . is not the special province of particular roles" (p. 269). This work is reviewed by York-Barr and Duke (2004) by highlighting four distinct areas of leadership, as follows:

- *Participative leadership*. Citing Leithwood and Duke (1999), York-Barr and Duke (2004) define *participative leadership* as involving the decision-making process: "One school of thought within this category of leadership argues for such participation on the grounds that it will enhance organizational effectiveness. A second school rests its case for participation on democratic principles" (Leithwood & Duke, 1999, p. 51, as cited by York-Barr & Duke, 2004, p. 261).

Reflective Question

1. What is the relationship among participation, collaboration, and democracy within a school context as opposed to a political process?

• *Leadership as organizational quality*. Rather than focusing on individual initiatives, accentuate organizational work. Teacher leadership must be seen within a larger social or institutional context. "The leadership must affect more than individuals' actions; it must influence the system in which actions occur" (Ogawa & Bossert, 1995, p. 233, as cited by York-Barr & Duke, 2004, p. 262).

Reflective Question

1. How do you accomplish leadership on an institutional rather than an individual basis? Provide a concrete example.

• *Distributed leadership*. Introduced by Spillane et al. (2001), the concept of distributed leadership reflects a commitment to encourage collaboration around leadership opportunities schoolwide. *Distributed leadership* is a concept that Richard Elmore (1999) has extended to explain how real instructional improvement takes place: It is

> change with direction, sustained over time, that moves entire systems, raising the average level of quality and performance, while at the same time decreasing the variation among units, and engaging people in analysis and understanding of why some actions seem to work and others don't. (p. 24)

He also believes that it is only through "distributed leadership," and not the more common, romanticized conception of the charismatic or heroic leader, that this type of improvement can succeed. The work of the leader is to organize the diverse competencies of the people in schools into a coherent whole so that the knowledge and skill of one person complements those of another, competencies are shared, and additional needed competencies are brought into the organization (Elmore, 1999). It is a coherent set of goals that give meaning and direction to the learning and collegiality that the leader fosters. Collegiality is not effective without connection to a strong congruence among values, norms, behaviors, and goals of principals and teachers (Rosenholtz, 1986).

Reflective Question

1. What does distributed leadership mean to you as a collaborative leader?

- *Parallel leadership.* This concept, developed by Crowther, Kaagen, Ferguson, and Hann (2002), equates the important work of both administrators and teachers, albeit in different ways. Although principals and teachers both work toward the same general goal, principals may focus on strategic planning, resource allocations, and visioning, while teachers focus on instructional leadership related to pedagogy within classrooms. Emphasizing different tasks, they still can collaborate by sharing experiences with each other.

Reflective Question

1. How might parallel leadership contribute to collaboration in your school?

What do teacher leaders do? Research suggests that "leadership practices and possibilities for teachers are numerous and varied" (York-Barr & Duke, 2004, p. 263). Specifically, they may serve as committee chairpersons, department heads, coaches, mentors, union representatives, or members on schoolwide leadership teams. York-Barr and Duke review the literature and identify seven domains of practice in answer to the question "What do teacher leaders do?":

- Coordination/management—for example, coordinating schedules, participating in meetings
- School or district curriculum work—for example, textbook reviews, curriculum development
- Professional development of colleagues—for example, mentoring colleagues, conducting workshops, peer coaching
- Participation in school change/improvement—for example, action research, shared decision making
- Parent and community involvement—for example, encouraging parental involvement, working with local businesses
- Contributions to the profession—for example, members of local, state, or national organizations; union workers
- Preservice teacher education—for example, participating in Professional Development Schools, serving as cooperating teachers

Reflective Question

1. How might you as principal encourage or foster teacher leadership?

How can principals promote teacher leadership? York-Barr and Duke (2004) compile various suggestions from the literature:

- Build a school culture and environment that is conducive to teacher leadership, including both formal structures and informal behaviors.
- Provide expert leadership, relinquish authority, trust teachers, empower teachers, include others, protect teacher leaders from their colleagues, share responsibility for failure, and give credit for success.

- Redefine the role of the principal from instructional leader to developer of a community of leaders.
- Create opportunities for teachers to lead; build professional learning communities; provide quality, results-driven professional development; and celebrate innovation and teacher expertise.
- Provide a school environment in which teachers engage in reflective practice and can implement ideas that grow from reflection.
- Pay attention to the change process and to human relationships, listen well, communicate respect, perpetuate ongoing dialogue about teaching and learning, and encourage teachers to act on shared visions.
- Offer "diligent, supportive, visible, and frequent reinforcement of the real power of teacher leaders" (pp. 273–274).

As principal, you can do much to encourage teacher leadership. By providing time for teacher involvement (e.g., released time), you do much to demonstrate your true commitment. Providing work space, too, is essential. Teachers are too often isolated from each other physically. Providing a special room dedicated to collaborative team meetings symbolically and practically communicates a commitment to teacher leadership. Giving teachers access to material and financial resources is also critical. Further, the extent to which you clearly articulate a definition of roles and responsibilities for teacher leadership will determine the degree of teacher participation in schoolwide activities (i.e., instructional, curricular, administrative). As principal, you play the critical role "in the success of teacher leadership by actively supporting the development of teachers, by maintaining open channels of communication, and by aligning structures and resources to support the leadership work of teachers" (York-Barr & Duke, 2004, p. 288).

2. SITE-BASED MANAGEMENT

Chances for teacher leadership to emerge and be sustained increase when principals establish a site-based management structure in their schools. Teacher leadership that supports an overall commitment to collaboration does not occur in a vacuum or simply because a principal wants it to occur. Structures to support such activities must be established. One of these structures that by itself is closely aligned with collaborative leadership is site-based management. This structure found some popularity in the 1980s and 1990s (Conley, 1991) and is now reemerging as an important way to foster collaboration for whole-school improvement (York-Barr & Duke, 2004).

Let's first present a scenario, based on a real situation (Glanz, 1992) in which site-based management had severe limitations.

School-Based Management at P.S. X

P.S. X is located in the Flatbush section of Brooklyn, New York. It was built in 1905 and is a large elementary school serving approximately 1,500 pupils (kindergarten through grade 5). The school is administered by a principal and two assistant principals. It was identified, in the 1990s, by the New York State Department of Education as a school "in need of assistance" as a result of low scores in reading at the third-grade level. The pupil ethnic census provided the following data about the school's student population: African American, 85%; Hispanic American, 10%; Asian American, 3%; and other, 2%. The socioeconomic data indicated that 95% of the students were eligible this year for free lunch. Also, P.S. X is a Title I school.

P.S. X was selected as a school to participate in site-based management because it was a school designated by the state for review. Initial apprehension by teachers and administrators alike was not uncommon. Frequent comments were: "What does all this mean?" "Who's in charge?" "Will we get support from the district office, state?" "Who will be directly involved in decision making—all teachers or a representative committee?" "What role will the principal and his assistants have in making decisions?" and "Who's accountable?" Although the faculty and staff did not volunteer to participate in the Site-Based Management/Shared Decision Making (SBM/SDM) model, there was remarkable consensus among faculty that this was a unique opportunity to help children succeed. District and state experts explained the program to school members, and a committee (comprised initially of volunteers) was formed early in the school year. With the full cooperation of the administrative team, a committee of teachers, parents, and administrators met on a regular basis. The administration at P.S. X always believed that decisions were more effective when achieved through collaboration. They believed that this plan, sponsored by the New York City schools' chancellor at the time, would expand efforts already underway at the school to involve teachers and parents more meaningfully. They believed that shared decision making through, for example, teacher advisory councils enhanced the feeling of ownership of the decisions that affected the school. Although the administration assumed responsibility for what happened in the school, decisions made collaboratively resulted in greater teacher commitment as well as ensuring that implementation of decisions occurred.

I have elsewhere described the efforts of P.S. X to implement SBM/SDM (Glanz, 1992). Ultimately, however, the path toward shared governance was not a smooth one. Administrators and teachers alike encountered a number of critical problems. Although teachers and administrators collaborated on a number of projects, these successful efforts were short-lived. Sustained efforts at collaboration became less frequent. Some specific problems centered around initial unwillingness of teachers to assume responsibility for important decisions. In one major instance, a committee, primarily of teachers, was given authority, or so they thought, to spend $1.5 million of discretionary funds on curricular and instructional materials; however, they were reluctant, ultimately, to assume responsibility. Teachers quietly asked, "Will we personally be held responsible for misappropriations or misused funds?" One teacher simply said, "Let the principal decide." Teachers did not receive much guidance for decision making, nor were they trained to work together on a larger scale. Roland Barth (1988) put it this way, "Through what alchemy is a disparate, sometimes desperate, group of individuals, accustomed to trying to have it their own way in a small

> domain, going to learn to work together in the best interests of the larger domain?" (p. 23).
>
> Administrators in the school were a bit reluctant to relinquish decision-making authority. (Parenthetically, this scenario represents a "top-down" model of collaboration, i.e., initiated by mandate from a district office.) In fact, when the committee ultimately gave their recommendations to the principal for spending the money, he changed many of their allocations to suit what he thought was best. When word got out that he had made these alterations in budgetary matters, teachers, who had participated for a period of four months, voiced dissatisfaction, some vowing never again to volunteer for such a committee. "What sense does it make," said one teacher, "spending all that time so that in the end the principal could simply make his decision without regard to ours?!" School-based management ultimately failed at P.S. X.

To what can we attribute the fall of SBM/SDM in this school? In addition to the reasons implicit above, reform cannot take place in a haphazard, piecemeal fashion. Systemic change is necessary to mitigate bureaucratic influences that hinder participatory management and successful schooling. School-based management as a one-shot reform effort at the school level is destined to fail without broad institutional support (Fullan, 1999). Further, Fullan's (1999) discussion of the need for balance between top-down and bottom-up change seems relevant here as well.

Although research confirms the fact that participation at all levels is associated with positive outcomes, such as greater staff morale, organizational commitment, and a reduction of conflict (see, e.g., Blase & Kirby, 1992; Kochan, Katz, & Mower, 1985; Nadler, 1986; Sashkin, 1984), teacher participation alone is not an assurance that positive changes are inevitable (Porter, Lawler, & Hackman, 1975). Teacher participation is successful only to the extent that other intervening and contextual variables are set in motion (Shedd, 1987). As Conley, Schmidle, and Shedd (1988) explain: "When employees have the formal authority to make decisions, but their actual discretion is tightly circumscribed by prescribed agenda, organizational norms, resource limitations, or similar factors, the purported benefits of participation strategies are often minimal or nonexistent" (p. 260). In other words, teacher participation alone does not necessarily eliminate or even mitigate bureaucratic influences. An organizational effort is necessary to ensure that pedagogical, curricular, and administrative strategies work in consonance with participatory management.

Reflective Question

1. What could (or would) you do to ensure a more successful result to site-based management in your school? Describe specific strategies and activities.

The following suggestions, among others, may serve to support site-based management, collaboration, and shared decision making:

- *Assess your commitment.* Are you truly interested in bringing others into decision-making processes?
- *Collaborate with others to develop goals.* Have you collaboratively articulated goals and objectives? In other words, what's the purpose for collaborating? To achieve what?
- *Build trust and rapport.* Have you established a conducive, nonthreatening environment in which to conduct deliberations?
- *Open lines of communication.* Have you ensured that all interested parties have received notifications or updates via memorandum, e-mail, or otherwise?
- *Set in place conflict resolution strategies.* Do you anticipate that disagreements may occur? What mechanisms are in place to deal with them?
- *Get involved.* Have you made sure you are highly visible, cordial, and knowledgeable? Have you established the committee and then "disappeared"?
- *Articulate roles, responsibilities, and relationships.* Have respect, clear guidelines, and a chain of command been established and understood by all parties?
- *Keep everyone in the loop.* Are you honest and up-front with everyone regarding potential risks and opportunities?

- *Put into place professional development on an ongoing basis, as necessary.* Have you considered the use of professional development activities to assist committee members in communication skills, conflict resolution, consensus building, and so forth?
- *Specify parameters for shared decision making.* Are all parties clear on "who" makes the decisions and how they are made?
- *Provide time and a place for meetings.* Have you established the necessary time and space structures that are so necessary for collaboration to take place?
- *Establish incentives and rewards.* Have you considered the types of positive reinforcement participants want, need, and expect?
- *Identify leadership roles.* Have you considered leadership styles in committee formation and carrying out of responsibilities?
- *Identify opportunities for more collaboration.* What other opportunities for leadership and decision making can you encourage teachers and others to engage in?
- *Always listen.* Do you get out there to listen to complaints as much as you do successes?
- *Form internal alliances.* Are you aware of cliques that may form that may interfere or support a committee or team's work?
- *Form external alliances.* What connections can you make with the community to support internal collaborative work?
- *Keep student learning in mind.* Are you continually aware of why collaboration is so important?

Reflective Questions

1. To what extent can you implement the previous suggestions?
2. What other suggestions can you offer?

CONCLUSION

Collaborative leadership does not occur in a vacuum and is not in the sole purview of a principal. An important prerequisite to meaningful and successful collaboration is empowering teachers by enhancing their own leadership potential within schools. Site-based management is the kind of structure that facilitates or makes possible teacher involvement or collaborative leadership.

> *"All successful change processes are characterized by collaboration and close interaction among those central to carrying out the changes. . . . Alliances provide greater power, both of ideas and the ability to act on them."*
>
> —Michael Fullan

As primary collaborative leader in the school, you set the tone for all collaboration that follows. It's your beliefs and actions that form the foundation for schoolwide collaboration. You encourage, support, and sustain teacher leadership within a site-based managed structure because of the following reasons, among others:

- Collaboration, like leadership in general, is a responsibility, obligation, and moral commitment of the many.
- Schools are too complex today for any single individual to make a difference on a systemic, institutional level.
- Promoting student achievement is a schoolwide goal.
- The more individuals are committed to a project or goal, the greater the likelihood it will succeed.
- It's the right thing to do.

Conclusion

Making Collaborative Leadership a Reality

"Creating a collegial culture within a learning community includes the following interactive and critical elements: mutual respect, conversations about teaching and learning, shared values and vision, clear expectations, time to share, teamwork, professional development, inquiry, and reflective practice."

—Marsha Speck

"Collaborations are the vehicles for those of us who believe we can make a difference."

—Hank Rubin

Collaborative leadership is not a luxury but a necessity. Principals by themselves cannot solve the complex problems confronting schools today. The ability to bring together a group of diverse individuals committed to the greater, common good of the school is essential for today's principal. Collaborative leadership involves building a cadre of concerned professionals committed to working together as a cooperative team to address various curricular, instructional, and other school-related issues. "Buy-in," by teachers and parents, for instance, is critical given the history of educational reform (e.g., Cuban, 1984; Elmore,

1999), which has been lackluster, top-driven, and ephemeral. Some principals eschew collaboration by saying, "Well, my teachers are not interested in participating in decision making." First, one may question the principal's commitment to facilitating such an effort; and second, it is a mistake to have as a goal *total* teacher commitment to collaborative decision making. Start small, and build that cadre. I always try to keep Margaret Mead's inspiring admonition in mind (I paraphrase): "Never doubt that a small group of committed individuals can change the world, for indeed it is the only thing that ever has."

If one asks most principals if they are committed to collaboration, they are likely to give you a strange look and say, "Of course." Most educators are aware that collaboration is essential. But if one queries some of these principals more deeply, one discovers what they really mean by *collaboration.* Here are a few examples taken from interviews I've conducted with a number of principals:

- "My teachers work with me . . . whenever they can."
- "My teachers are busy . . . but they try."
- "Certainly, I solicit input from my teachers whenever I need to purchase a new curriculum material."
- "My parents are involved. They contribute to our annual bake sale; they are here every day in the office I set aside for them."

Upon closer scrutiny to each of these comments, one discovers the superficial nature of the collaboration that exists. Establishing conditions that facilitate and encourage participation is only minimally accomplished. When collaboration does occur, it usually involves petty or insignificant matters. And when it does occur, it's usually temporary and episodic. The kind of collaboration we have discussed and encouraged in this volume is much more profound and meaningful. It means going out of one's way to ensure that most teachers and parents, for instance, contribute to meaningful matters such as major curricular innovations, curricular expenditures, instructional materials, professional development programs, and even hiring, where feasible. Encouraging and sustaining teacher leadership and shared decision making as fundamental to a principal's, a school's, success are imperative if "true collaboration," in the words of Hargreaves and Dawe (1989) cited earlier in this volume, is to occur. Such collaboration is deep, sustained, and engrained in the everyday work of both principals and teachers.

A sensible approach to shared decision making was recently offered by Rooney (2004). He explains that we need to consider the "different kinds of input and action" (p. 85) we want. Spontaneous decisions must obviously be made by the principal alone. As we mentioned earlier, situations such as fire drills do not require collaboration. He states, "We need not call for consensus on indoor recess when it is pouring rain" (p. 85). His approach is further addressed:

> Other times, I needed a bit of advice. Hiring staff, although ultimately my decision, occurred only after teachers had interviewed, discussed, and recommended candidates. I often asked my secretary to listen to ideas and give me feedback. My PTA president edited my newsletters to save me from "edubabble." Our special education teacher acted as the informal staff ombudsman. When something was amiss, she came into my office, looked me straight in the eye, and gave me the honest feedback.
>
> Like democracy, such a system of decision making is not always efficient. Learning which decisions are "mine," which are "ours," and which are "theirs" is a process of trial and error. But by gathering the collective wisdom of staff members, this system ends up being more effective. After all, we entrust teachers each and every day with our kids—our most cherished responsibilities. We must also trust teachers to make the organizational decisions that affect their own lives and the lives of students. (p. 85)

Collaborative leadership, therefore, is inclusive. It's about welcoming different points of view and reaching consensus, if possible. Collaborative leadership is not easy. Most educators are not used to collaboration, given the bureaucratic-hierarchical legacy in the field of education. As principal, you must take the leadership initiative to reach out to others. You must build and sustain the institutional mechanisms to ensure that collaboration works. You must be willing to listen to others, value their views, and be willing to compromise. Collaboration occurs over time, in slow, deliberative ways. It is no magic bullet. But when done correctly, collaborative leadership contributes to a team effort aimed at ensuring that the education occurring in a school is of the highest quality.

Resource A

Realities of Collaborative Leadership: In-Basket Simulations

This section highlights some of the realities of collaborative leadership using an approach called "In-Basket Simulations." It is a study technique derived from an approach used when I studied for licensure as a principal in New York City. The approach was developed by the Institute for Research and Professional Development (http://www.nycenet.edu/opm/opm/profservices/rfp1b723.html). Scenarios that you as a principal might encounter are presented for your reaction. For instance, "A letter from an irate parent complaining that her child is intentionally being ignored during instruction in class by the teacher is sent to your attention. What would you do?" Challenging you to confront real-life phenomena under controlled conditions, these simulated in-basket items will prompt critical inquiry.

Here are suggestions to guide you as you complete these in-basket exercises:

1. Think and respond as if you are a principal, not a teacher or an assistant principal.
2. Place yourself mentally in each situation as if the case were actually happening to you.
3. Draw on your experiences and from what you've learned from others. Think of a principal you respect, and ask yourself, "What would Mr. or Ms. X have done?"
4. Make distinctions between actions you would personally take and actions you would delegate to others.

5. Utilize resources (personnel or otherwise) to assist you.
6. Think about your response, and then share it with a colleague for her or his reaction.
7. Record your response, and then a day later reread the scenario and your response. Would you still have reacted the same way?

(Please note that other books provide longer case studies that serve as an excellent way of reflecting on moral dilemmas. Refer to Maxcy [2002], Strike, Haller, & Soltis [2005], and Zubay & Soltis [2005].)

During an interview, you are asked to respond to the following scenarios:

• You are a newly appointed principal to an intermediate school in which the former principal was an autocrat. You want to encourage collaboration among teachers, but there's resistance. What are the first steps you'd take?

• Your superintendent informs you that she doesn't like the fact that you're encouraging shared decision making regarding personnel matters. How would you convince the superintendent that such decision making is critical to your role as principal?

• Two members on a school leadership team monopolize committee time with their incessant babbling, often off topic. The team leader is meek and will not confront them. The matter has reached your attention. What would you do, if anything?

• You want to initiate an action research project to address failing writing scores in grade 5. No one on staff knows much about action research, although you do. How would you go about establishing an action research team and project?

• You've formed a decision-making curriculum committee who reports that they would like to purchase a specific book series for grade 6. The committee members, having done their research, feel strongly about their decision. You've had previous experience with this book series while you were an assistant principal in another district. From your experience, you've noticed several severe limitations of the series. What would you do?

- You've formed a leadership committee that has, in the past, functioned quite well. After the most recent faculty elections, two new members join the committee. You notice, and hear from others, that arguments are now common in most meetings. What would you do or suggest?

- You're a newly assigned principal to a high school that never experienced teacher leadership, to any significant degree, nor shared decision making. You want to establish a collaborative school environment. What would be your two-year plan to achieve your goal?

- You've successfully implemented shared decision making involving instructional and curricular matters. The leadership team informs you that they now would like decision-making power over personnel matters as well. How would you react?

Resource B

Assessing Your Role in Teamwork

As the principal, you realize that collaboration requires people working together as a unit. Teamwork requires commitment on your part and that of each member. Please complete this questionnaire as a means of self-reflection or analysis in order to assess the extent to which you share collaborative aspirations. You realize, of course, that the survey is not scientific, and results therefore should be studied in that light. Please note that your responses are private. Your honest responses to the various items below will best serve as reflective tools to assist you in becoming an even better collaborative leader.

SA = Strongly Agree ("For the most part, yes.")
A = Agree ("Yes, but . . .")
D = Disagree ("No, but . . .")
SD = Strongly Disagree ("For the most part, no.")

SA A D SD 1. I am willing to listen to and learn from others.

SA A D SD 2. I am willing to alter my views after deliberating with others, if their views are more convincing.

SA A D SD 3. I am willing to let go of a firmly held belief in order to reach consensus with others.

SA A D SD 4. Although I am ultimately responsible for what happens in my school, I believe that responsibility is a shared goal of the entire team.

SA A D SD 5. I intentionally serve as a collaborative leader.

SA A D SD 6. If every other member of the team votes for "X" but I really believe in "Y," I would still go along with the team if I could not convince them otherwise.

SA A D SD 7. I am willing to relinquish my authority for the good of a team concept.

SA A D SD 8. Team members should like one another.

SA A D SD 9. Everyone on a team should participate.

SA A D SD 10. My role on the team is to ensure that conflict is minimized.

SA A D SD 11. Establishing clear goals and roles for each member is imperative.

SA A D SD 12. Team-building activities should be used to establish good working relationships among team members.

SA A D SD 13. Consensus is a much better way of reaching a conclusion than voting.

SA A D SD 14. A team member should always remain on a team even when personal conflicts reach crisis proportions.

SA A D SD 15. Collaboration is among the most important things I do as principal.

Analyze your responses:

The "answers" below are suggestive, because no survey can accurately assess your commitment to collaboration. However, the responses below can serve as a basis of comparison and as a means of reflection by yourself or with a colleague.

An affirmative response to the following items is clearly necessary if collaboration is going to work in your school: 1 through 7, 11 through 13, and 15. Response to #8—not necessarily "like" but, rather, "get along" is more appropriate. Response to #10—not that conflict is minimized but perhaps managed well. Response to #14—not necessarily; sometimes realignment is necessary.

Let's analyze each response more closely:

1. If you are not willing to listen and learn, you will not succeed as a collaborative leader. The days when the principal served as autocrat, if that ever worked, are long gone.

2 and 3. A principal who is confident and has a strong belief system would be willing to alter his or her views. Doing so would not be seen as a diminishment of authority or of person. Rather, it is a sign of maturity and commitment to the larger good.

4. A principal genuinely committed to collaboration would hold such a view. Clearly, some principals might say they're collaborative, but they are willing to go only so far. How far are you willing to go? What are your limits, if any? These questions are very important for you to reflect upon and share with a colleague for deeper discussion.

5 and 15. A collaborative leader would undoubtedly affirm these statements.

6 and 7. These really test your "limits" for collaboration. Consider carefully by thinking of the consequences of your actions. Commitment to collaboration for some of you may not be an either-or proposition. Shades of gray are possible. Where do you stand on the authoritarian/collaborative continuum?

8. Although desirable, liking each other personally is not as important as being willing to professionally cooperate for a greater good.

9. Participation on a committee is voluntary. However, everyone should be afforded opportunity to participate. How can you do so?

10. It's difficult to "control" for conflict. Conflict is inevitable. Your role is to ensure that conflicts do not get to the point that the team cannot conduct its work. Well-managed conflict can move the group toward positive results.

11. Usually, setting clear goals and roles is wise. At other times, it may be best for the team to meet and see where things go. Roles sometimes develop naturally through deliberation. Organizational, team, and individual goals should be aligned.

12. Yes, read Chapter 2.

13. Yes; voting results in winners and losers. In consensus, everyone wins. Yet consensus building is time-consuming and can lead, at times, to a watered-down decision. A watered-down decision, however, may be better than one not derived through the combined efforts of all.

14. No, there are times when certain team members should be asked to leave when their presence only exacerbates problems to the point that the team cannot function.

Reflective Questions

1. How might you use the survey and the explanations to assess your personal commitment to collaboration?
2. What insights into teamwork have you gained from this exercise?
3. Examine each item and corresponding statement, and explain how you intend to actively change your behavior in order to best promote a sense of collaboration and teamwork.

Resource C

Assessing Your Role in Action Research

This questionnaire is a bit different from the others in this volume and series in that it assesses your knowledge of action research very specifically or technically. You can, of course, support action research initiatives, as principal, without having specialized expertise in the area, but having some basic knowledge and experience in actually conducting it is more likely to strengthen your commitment. Please complete this questionnaire as a means of self-reflection or analysis in order to assess the extent to which you are knowledgeable of the action research process. Note that the questionnaire stresses knowledge that is not matched to the content of this book; it's just meant to prompt you to think about what you know or may not know about research specifics. You know, though, that it is really only "doing" action research a bit that will assist you to gain greater familiarity and knowledge. Please note that the questions posed do not cover all areas of action research. The intent is to conduct some rudimentary assessment. Refer to any good text on educational or action research for details (see Resource E in this book). Please also note that your responses are private. Your honest responses to the various items below will best serve as reflective tools to assist you in becoming an even better collaborative leader.

1. Which of the following is an example of empirical research?

   a. A study of the impact of a literature-based reading series on the attitudes of fifth graders toward reading
   b. A review of the literature on cooperative learning

c. A historical overview of homeschooling
d. All of these are examples of empirical research

2. Which is an example of an ethnographic study?

a. Images of principals in the media
b. Relationship between math and science scores among 11th graders
c. A day in the life of a local school superintendent
d. Programmed textbook instruction versus computer-assisted instruction

3. Mr. Solomon is a principal in an elementary school. Mr. Jones, a sixth-grade teacher, complains that one student, Billy, is disruptive and recalcitrant. Mr. Solomon tells the teacher to record Billy's behavior in anecdotal form for two weeks before scheduling a conference with the guidance counselor. During the first week, Mr. Jones discovers that Billy acts out 26 times. During the second week, he acts out 22 times. During the third week, Mr. Jones meets with the guidance counselor to work out Billy's problems. The counselor sets up a special reward system for Billy. During the fourth week, Billy acts out 18 times. During the fifth week, the disturbances decrease to only five times. Mr. Jones and the counselor conclude that the technique used with Billy is successful. What research design was employed?

a. Pretest-posttest control group design
b. Control group–only design
c. Interrupted time series design
d. Single measurement design
e. Nonequivalent control group design

4. Mrs. James teaches computers at P.S. 999. She has a new programmed instruction textbook that she wishes to use with her classes. She decides to test the effectiveness of the new textbook. She chooses two classes that rank similarly in ability on a pretest in computer literacy. She gives her programmed text to group A, but with group B she continues her normal instruction. At the end of the semester, she gives a test on computer knowledge and discovers that the class using the new text outperformed the other group (group B). She

concludes that the new text should be incorporated in all the classes. What research design did Mrs. James use?

a. Nonequivalent design
b. Interrupted time series design
c. Pretest-posttest design
d. Pretest-posttest control group design
e. Control group–only design

5. You take 50 fourth-grade students and assign 25 randomly to one class and 25 randomly to the other class. Both groups are measured beforehand. Two different treatments are presented, then a follow-up measurement is given. Which type of design is this?

a. Pretest-posttest control group design
b. Pretest-posttest only design
c. One-shot case study
d. Nonequivalent control group design
e. One-group pretest-posttest design

6. A quasi-experimental design involving one group that is repeatedly pretested, exposed to an experimental treatment, and repeatedly posttested is known as a

a. Pretest-posttest design
b. Posttest-only design
c. Time-series design
d. Revolving series design
e. None of these

7. Classify the following study:

Research hypothesis: Achievement in Spanish is affected by class size.

Procedure: At the beginning of the school year, the students in Highpoint High School are randomly assigned to one of two types of Spanish classes: a class with 20 or fewer students or a class of 40 or more. The two groups are compared at the end of the year on Spanish achievement.

a. Historical
b. Descriptive

c. Correlational
d. Experimental

8. Janice Barnett, Supervisor of Curriculum, wanted to evaluate a new reading series that her district was considering. She decided to study fifth graders in a particular school. She selected one class of fifth-grade students who were introduced to the new reading series. Another comparable fifth-grade class would use the "old" reading series. At the end of the year, Ms. Barnett tested all students in reading comprehension. What type of study is this?

   a. Pretest-posttest control group
   b. Nonequivalent
   c. Case study
   d. Historical

9. To determine if a particular textbook is appropriate for a fifth-grade class, your analysis would entail which type of research?

   a. Content analysis
   b. Ethnography
   c. Case study
   d. Naturalism
   e. Simulation

10. The major purpose of using an interview protocol is to:

    a. Offer respondents a way to participate in the interview without having the interviewer present
    b. Increase the chances that the respondent will respond honestly
    c. Be able to conduct the interview in case the interviewer is not present
    d. Provide the interviewer with a set of guidelines for conducting the interview

11. You are a principal in an intermediate school with a population of 750 students. As indicated by recent districtwide tests, student reading achievement has increased. You are interested in discovering how well the students in your school

perform in reading compared to students in other schools throughout the country. Which of the following instruments of measurement would you use?

a. A classroom achievement test
b. Observation
c. Examination of school records
d. A questionnaire
e. A standardized test

12. When a group of subjects (experimental) sense that they are part of an experiment and react in a special way it is known as the

a. John Henry effect
b. Norton's Law
c. Halo effect
d. Hawthorne effect
e. Pearson *r*

13. This is an ethical principle related to conducting research that ensures that participants in research are informed accurately about the general topic under investigation as well as any unusual procedures that may be used in the study.

a. Accurate disclosure
b. Fair-mindedness
c. Ethics
d. Beneficence

14. This occurs when subjects in the control group know they are, in a sense, competing with some other group (experimental) and, consequently, expend extra effort to perform better than the experimental group.

a. Hawthorne effect
b. John Henry effect
c. Western Electric effect
d. John James effect
e. All of the above

15. Participant observation is frequently used in conducting

a. Correlational research
b. Ex post facto research

c. Ethnographic research
d. Quasi-experimental research

16. A research hypothesis should be stated in the form of a

a. Value judgment
b. Hypothetical construct
c. Research question
d. Predictive statement

17. The degree to which a test consistently measures whatever it measures is

a. Reliability
b. Validity
c. Coefficient
d. Statistical analysis
e. None of these

18. Which of the following is the best example of an "unobtrusive instrument"?

a. Supervisor walks into class for an on-the-spot observation
b. Supervisor peeks into window of classroom without letting the teacher see him or her
c. Supervisor determines staff morale by examining the quantity and pattern of staff attendance
d. Interviewing teachers
e. Anonymous questionnaire

19. Internal validity is to accuracy of results as external validity is to

a. Threats to validity
b. Causality realities
c. Triangulation
d. Generalizability

20. What should be your first reaction when you hear a radio commentator report that a recently published article indicates that a particular drug may reduce the risks for cancer?

a. Disbelieve the study
b. Accept it as accurate

c. Assume that it's a PR push by a pharmaceutical company
d. Consider study limitations

21. Action research differs most from typical professional practice in its

a. Concern for fostering students' learning
b. Concern for discovering generalizable knowledge
c. Promotion of practitioners' professional development
d. Systematic collection of data as a guide to improving practice

22. List five benefits of conducting action research.

23. List the four basic steps of conducting action research.

24. List the three forms of action research.

25. List some practical guidelines or advice you'd give others for conducting action research.

ANSWERS: 1, a; 2, c; 3, c; 4, a; 5, a; 6, c; 7, d; 8, b; 9, a; 10, d; 11, e; 12, d; 13, a; 14, b; 15, c; 16, d; 17, a; 18, c; 19, d; 20, d; 21, d; 22 through 25, consult Chapter 3.

Reflective Questions

1. How might you use the survey and the explanations to assess your personal knowledge of action research?
2. What insights into action research have you gained from this exercise?
3. How might you gain more knowledge of action research?

Resource D

Assessing Your Role in Shared Decision Making

As the principal, you realize that shared decision making deepens a sense of collaboration. Shared decision making requires commitment on your part and that of each member of the committee, group, or team. Please complete this questionnaire as a means of self-reflection or analysis in order to assess the extent to which you are willing to share decision making. You realize, of course, that the survey is not scientific, and results therefore should be studied in that light. Please note that your responses are private. Your honest responses to the various items below will best serve as reflective tools to assist you in becoming an even better collaborative leader.

SA = Strongly Agree ("For the most part, yes.")
A = Agree ("Yes, but . . .")
D = Disagree ("No, but . . .")
SD = Strongly Disagree ("For the most part, no.")

SA A D SD 1. I am in favor of building a school culture and environment that is conducive to teacher leadership, including both formal structures and informal behaviors.

SA A D SD 2. I am willing to relinquish authority, trust teachers, empower teachers, include others, protect teacher leaders from their colleagues, share responsibility for failure, and give credit for success.

SA A D SD 3. I believe that the role of the principal should be redefined from instructional leader to developer of a community of leaders.

SA A D SD 4. I intend to create opportunities for teachers to lead; build professional learning communities; provide quality, results-driven professional development; and celebrate innovation and teacher expertise.

SA A D SD 5. I will provide for a school environment in which teachers engage in reflective practice and can implement ideas that grow from reflection.

SA A D SD 6. I will pay attention to the change process and to human relationships, listen well, communicate respect, perpetuate ongoing dialogue about teaching and learning, and encourage teachers to act on shared visions.

SA A D SD 7. I will empower teachers as leaders.

SA A D SD 8. I am truly interested in bringing others into decision-making processes.

SA A D SD 9. I fully understand the purpose for collaborating.

SA A D SD 10. I will establish a conducive, nonthreatening environment in which to conduct decision-making deliberations.

SA A D SD 11. I will open lines of communication to all those interested in partaking in decision making.

SA A D SD 12. I am ready, willing, and able to introduce, when needed, conflict resolution strategies.

SA A D SD 13. I will be highly visible, cordial, and knowledgeable in regard to shared decision making.

SA A D SD 14. I intend to establish the necessary time and space structures that are so necessary for collaboration to take place.

SA A D SD 15. I remain committed to shared decision making as a way to support collaboration in my school.

Analyze your responses:

The "answers" below are suggestive, because no survey can accurately assess your commitment to shared decision making. However, the responses below can serve as a basis of comparison and as a means of reflection by yourself or with a colleague.

Affirmative answers to the first seven questions indicate your commitment to building, encouraging, and sustaining teacher leadership.

Affirmative answers to the remaining eight questions demonstrate your commitment to shared decision making.

Reflective Questions

1. How might you use the survey and the explanations to assess your personal commitment to shared decision making?
2. What insights into shared decision making have you gained from this exercise?
3. Examine each item and corresponding statement, and explain how you intend to actively change your behavior in order to best promote a sense of collaboration and shared decision making.

Resource E

An Annotated Bibliography of Best Resources

The literature on the principalship and related areas is extensive. The list below is not meant to serve as a comprehensive resource by any means. The selected titles I have annotated are few but, in my opinion, are among the most useful references on the subject. Rater than "impress" you with a more extensive list, I have selected these outstanding works related specifically to collaborative leadership that will supplement my book quite well. I may have missed, of course, other important works. Nevertheless, the list below is a good start. Don't forget that life is a long journey of continuous learning. Continue to hone your skills by reading good books and journal articles on collaborative leadership. No one is ever perfect, and everyone can learn something new by keeping current with the literature in the field. Share your readings and reactions with a colleague.

Action Research

Ferance, E. (2000). *Action research.* Providence, RI: Northeast and Islands Regional Educational Laboratory at Brown University.

Very brief booklet that serves as a superb primer.

Glanz, J. (2003). *Action research: An educational leader's guide to school improvement* (2nd ed.). Norwood, MA: Christopher-Gordon.

Tough to recommend one's own work, but what can I say?

Mills, G. (2002). *Action research: A guide for the teacher researcher.* Englewood Cliffs, NJ: Prentice Hall.

Wonderful text to offer teachers for their professional development. Also, good background for principals to become more familiar with action research.

Team Building

Biech, E. (Ed.). (2001). *The Pfeiffer book of successful team-building tools.* San Francisco: Jossey-Bass.

One of the most concise books on the topic. In a field that has many similar books, this volume is among the very best. Easy step-by-step activities to follow. Good theoretical background offered.

Glanz, J. (2002). *Finding your leadership style: A guide for educators.* Alexandria, VA: Association for Supervision and Curriculum Development.

There I go again. But it is a useful tool to assess individual leadership styles, so crucial for team building and learning.

Kroehnert, G. (1993). *100 training games.* New York: McGraw-Hill.

Stimulating role plays, engaging simulations, and practical exercises for improving communication skills, creating teamwork, learning perception skills, and so on.

Visit http://www.hrdq.com for a wealth of information on team building, leadership styles, coaching, conflict, and so forth.

Collaborative Leadership

Chrislip, D. D. (2002). *The collaborative leadership fieldbook.* San Francisco: Jossey-Bass.

Results oriented, comprehensive, and practical, this handbook is an excellent resource for a principal. Very well organized and laid out; easy to use.

Robbins, P., & Alvy, H. B. (2003). *The principal's companion: Strategies and hints to make the job easier* (2nd ed.). Thousand Oaks, CA: Corwin.

One of the best volumes on the principalship. Chapter 11, on building collaborative schools, is particularly informative.

Rubin, H. (2002). *Collaborative leadership: Developing effective partnerships in communities and schools.* Thousand Oaks, CA: Corwin.

Offers sound guidance on cultivating relationships within the school and with outside interests. Specific skills that foster collaboration are included. Aspects of this book informed this present volume a great deal.

Shared Decision Making

Reed, C. J. (2000). *Teaching with power: Shared decision-making and classroom practice.* New York: Teachers College Press.

Not many books out there specifically address this topic. This one, though, is a highly readable book based on practical experiences of involving teachers in decision making.

References

Adelman, C. (1993). Kurt Lewin and the origins of action research. *Educational Action Research, 1*(1), 7–24.

Ambrose, D., & Cohen, L. M. (1997). The post-industrial era: Finding the giftedness in all children. *Focus on Education, 41*, 20–23.

Barth, R. (1988). *Improving schools from within: Teachers, parents, and principals can make the difference.* San Francisco: Jossey-Bass.

Bennis, W. (1989). *On becoming a leader.* Reading, MA: Addison-Wesley.

Biech, E. (Ed.). (2001). *The Pfeiffer book of successful team-building tools.* San Francisco: Jossey-Bass.

Blase, J., & Kirby, P. C. (1992). *Bringing out the best in teachers: What effective principals do.* Thousand Oaks, CA: Corwin.

Bruckner, M. (2004). The passion to lead. *Education Update, 46*(7), 2.

Buckingham, M., & Clifton, D. O. (2001). *Now, discover your strengths.* New York: Free Press.

Calhoun, E. F. (1993). Action research: Three approaches. *Educational Leadership, 51*, 62–65.

Calhoun, E. F. (1994). *How to use action research in the self-renewing school.* Alexandria, VA: Association for Supervision and Curriculum Development.

Calhoun, E. F. (2002). Action research for school improvement. *Educational Leadership, 59*, 18–24.

Calhoun, E. F., Allen, L., Halliburton, C., & Jones, S. (1996, April). *Schoolwide action research: A study of facilitation.* Paper presented at the annual meeting of the American Educational Research Association, New York.

Cochran, K. F., DeRuiter, J. A., & King, R. A. (1993). Pedagogical content knowing: An integrative model for teacher preparation. *Journal of Teacher Education, 44*, 263–272.

Conley, S. (1991). Review of research on teacher participation in school decision making. In G. Grant (Ed.), *Review of research in education* (Vol. 17, pp. 225–265). Washington, DC: American Educational Research Association.

Conley, S. C., Schmidle, T., & Shedd, J. B. (1988). Teacher participation in the management of schools. *Teachers College Record, 90*, 245–278.

Corey, S. M. (1953). *Action research to improve school practices.* New York: Teachers College Press.

Cotton, K. (2003). *Principals and student achievement: What research says.* Alexandria, VA: Association for Supervision and Curriculum Development.

Crowther, F., Kaagen, S. S., Ferguson, M., & Hann, L. (2002). *Developing teacher leaders: How teacher leadership enhances school success.* Thousand Oaks, CA: Corwin.

Cuban, L. (1984). *How teachers taught: Constancy and change in American classrooms, 1890–1980.* New York: Longman.

Danielson, C. (2002). *Enhancing student achievement: A framework for school improvement.* Alexandria, VA: Association for Supervision and Curriculum Development.

Daresh, J. C. (1996, April). *Lessons for educational leadership from career preparation in law, medicine, and training for the priesthood.* Paper presented at the annual meeting of the American Educational Research Association, New York.

Duke, D. L. (1994). Drift, detachment, and the need for teacher leadership. In D. R. Walling (Ed.), *Teachers as leaders: Perspectives on the professional development of teachers* (pp. 255–273). Bloomington, IN: Phi Delta Kappa Educational Foundation.

Dunlap, D. M., & Goldman, P. (1991). Rethinking power in schools. *Educational Administration Quarterly, 27*(1), 5–29.

Elliott, J. (1991). *Action research for educational change.* Bristol, PA: Open University Press.

Elmore, R. (1999). *Leadership of large-scale improvement in American education.* Unpublished manuscript, Albert Shanker Institute, Washington, DC.

Fullan, M. (1995). Division I introduction—Contexts: Overview and framework. In M. J. O'Hair & S. J. Odell (Eds.), *Educating teachers for leadership and change* (pp. 1–10). Thousand Oaks, CA: Corwin.

Fullan, M. (1999). *Change forces: The sequel.* London: Falmer.

Glanz, J. (1992). School-based management and the advent of teacher empowerment: One administrator's view of reform. *Record in Educational Administration and Supervision, 12*, 40–45.

Glanz, J. (2002). *Finding your leadership style: A guide for educators.* Alexandria, VA: Association for Supervision and Curriculum Development.

Glanz, J. (2003). *Action research: An educational leader's guide to school improvement* (2nd ed.). Norwood, MA: Christopher-Gordon.

Glanz, J. (2005). Action research as instructional leadership: Suggestions for principals. *NASSP Bulletin, 89*(643), 17–27.

Glanz, J., & Sullivan, S. (2000). *Supervision in practice: Three steps to improve teaching and learning.* Thousand Oaks, CA: Corwin.

Glickman, C. D. (1998). *Renewing America's schools: A guide for school-based action.* San Francisco: Jossey-Bass.

Goodlad, J. I. (1994). *Educational renewal.* San Francisco: Jossey-Bass.

Hare, W. (1993). *What makes a good teacher: Reflections on some characteristics central to the educational enterprise.* London: Althouse.

Hargreaves, A., & Dawe, R. (1989, April). *Coaching as unreflective practice.* Paper presented at the American Educational Research Association Meeting, San Francisco.

Heck, R. H., Larsen, T. J., & Marcoulides, G. A. (1990). Instructional leadership and school achievement: Validation of a causal model. *Educational Administration Quarterly, 26*(2), 94–125.

Johnson, S. M. (1990). *Teachers at work: Achieving success in our schools.* New York: Basic Books.

Joyce, B., & Weil, M. (1999). *Models of teaching* (6th ed.). Boston: Allyn & Bacon.

Katz, M. B. (1987). *Restructuring American education.* Cambridge, MA: Harvard University Press.

Kirby, P. C. (1991, April). *Shared decision making: Moving from concerns about restrooms to concerns about classrooms.* Paper presented at the annual meeting of the American Educational Research Association, Chicago.

Kochan, T. A., Katz, H. C., & Mower, N. R. (1985). Worker participation and American unions. In T. A. Kochan (Ed.), *Challenges and choices facing American labor* (pp. 115–127). Cambridge: MIT Press.

Leithwood, K., Seashore Louis, K., Anderson, S., & Wahlstrom, K. (2004). *How leadership influences student learning.* Minneapolis: University of Minnesota, Center for Applied Research and Educational Improvement.

Lewin, K. (1948). *Resolving social conflicts.* New York: Harper and Brothers.

Marzano, R. J., Pickering, D. J., & Pollock, J. E. (2001). *Classroom instruction that works: Research-based strategies for increasing student achievement.* Alexandria, VA: Association for Supervision and Curriculum Development.

Maxcy, S. J. (2002). *Ethical school leadership.* Lanham, MD: Scarecrow Press.

Mills, G. (2002). *Action research: A guide for the teacher researcher.* Englewood Cliffs, NJ: Prentice Hall.

Moxley, R. S. (2000). *Leadership and spirit: Breathing new vitality and quality into individuals and organizations.* San Francisco: Jossey-Bass.

Nadelstern, E., Price, J. R., & Listhaus, A. (2000). Student empowerment through the professional development of teachers. In J. Glanz &

L. S. Behar-Horenstein (Eds.), *Paradigm debates in curriculum and supervision: Modern and postmodern perspectives* (pp. 265–275). Westport, CT: Bergin & Garvey.

Nadler, D. A. (1986). The effective management of organizational change. In J. W. Lorsch (Ed.), *Handbook of organizational behavior* (pp. 225–246). Englewood Cliffs, NJ: Prentice Hall.

Nieto, S. (2003). *Affirming diversity* (4th ed.). New York: Longman.

Noddings, N. (1984). *Caring: A feminist approach to ethics and moral education.* Berkeley: University of California Press.

Noddings, N. (1986). Fidelity in teaching, teacher education, and research for teaching. *Harvard Educational Review, 56*, 496–510.

Noddings, N. (1992). *The challenge to care in schools: An alternative approach to education.* New York: Teachers College Press.

Null, G. (1996). *Who are you, really? Understanding your life's energy.* New York: Carroll & Graf.

Oja, S., & Smulyan, L. (1989). *Collaborative action research: A developmental approach.* London: Falmer.

Osterman, K. F., & Kottkamp, R. B. (2004). *Reflective practice for educators: Improving schooling through professional development* (2nd ed.). Thousand Oaks, CA: Corwin.

Porter, L. W., Lawler, E. E., III, & Hackman, J. R. (1975). *Behavior in organizations.* New York: McGraw-Hill.

Robbins, P., & Alvy, H. B. (2003). *The principal's companion* (2nd ed.). Thousand Oaks, CA: Corwin.

Rooney, J. (2004). Sharing the decisions. *Educational Leadership, 62*(3), 84–85.

Rosenholtz, S. J. (1986). Organizational conditions of teacher learning. *Teaching and Teacher Education, 2*(2), 91–104.

Rubin, H. (2002). *Collaborative leadership: Developing effective partnerships in communities and schools.* Thousand Oaks, CA: Corwin.

Sagor, R. (1992). *How to conduct collaborative action research.* Alexandria, VA: Association for Supervision and Curriculum Development.

Sashkin, M. (1984). Participative management is an ethical imperative. *Organizational Dynamics, 12*, 5–22.

Schon, D. A. (1988). Coaching reflective teaching. In P. P. Grimmett & G. F. Erickson (Eds.), *Reflection in teacher education* (pp. 19–30). New York: Teachers College Press.

Sergiovanni, T. J. (1994). *Building community in schools.* San Francisco: Jossey-Bass.

Shedd, J. B. (1987). *Involving teachers in school and district decision-making.* New York: Organizational Analysis and Practice.

Sizer, T. R. (1984). *Horace's compromise: The dilemma of the American high school.* Boston: Houghton Mifflin.

Spillane, J. P., Halverson, R., & Diamond, J. B. (2001). Investigating school leadership practice: A distributed perspective. *Educational Researcher, 30*(3), 23–28.

Spring, J. (1992). *Images of American life: A history of ideological management in schools, movies, radio, and television.* Albany: State University of New York Press.

Strike, K. A., Haller, E. J., & Soltis, J. F. (2005). *The ethics of school administration* (3rd ed.). New York: Teachers College Press.

Stringer, E. T. (1996). *Action research: A handbook for practitioners.* Thousand Oaks, CA: Sage.

Sullivan, S., & Glanz, J. (2000). Alternative approaches to supervision: Cases from the field. *Journal of Curriculum and Supervision, 15,* 212–235.

Sullivan, S., & Glanz, J. (2005). *Supervision that improves teaching: Strategies and techniques* (2nd ed.). Thousand Oaks, CA: Corwin.

Taba, H., & Noel, E. (1957). *Action research: A case study.* Washington, DC: Association for Supervision and Curriculum Development.

Wilmore, E. L. (2002). *Principal leadership: Applying the new Educational Leadership Constituent Council (ELCC) standards.* Thousand Oaks, CA: Corwin.

York-Barr, J., & Duke, K. (2004). What do we know about teacher leadership? Findings from two decades of scholarship. *Review of Educational Research, 74,* 255–316.

Zepeda, S. (2003). *The principal as instructional leader: A handbook for supervisors.* Larchmont, NY: Eye on Education.

Zubay, B., & Soltis, J. (2005). *Creating the ethical school: A book of case studies.* New York: Teachers College Press.

Index

The Corwin Press logo—a raven striding across an open book—represents the union of courage and learning. Corwin Press is committed to improving education for all learners by publishing books and other professional development resources for those serving the field of PreK–12 education. By providing practical, hands-on materials, Corwin Press continues to carry out the promise of its motto: **"Helping Educators Do Their Work Better."**